中英双语版

企鹅经典 名人大发现

哈里·胡迪尼

[美]图伊·T. 萨瑟兰（Tui T.Sutherland）◎著 [美]约翰·奥布赖恩（John O'Brien）◎绘 曹幼南◎译

Who Was Harry Houdini?

CNS 湖南科学技术出版社 小博集 BOOKY KIDS
·长沙·

著作权合同登记号：字18-2024-198

图书在版编目（CIP）数据

名人大发现 ：哈里 · 胡迪尼 ：汉英对照 /（美）图伊 · T. 萨瑟兰（Tui T. Sutherland）著 ；曹幼南译 ；（美）约翰 · 奥布赖恩（John O'Brien）绘. -- 长沙 ：湖南科学技术出版社，2025. 1. --（企鹅经典）.
ISBN 978-7-5710-3268-5
Ⅰ. H319. 4
中国国家版本馆CIP数据核字第20245CH640号

上架建议：科普读物

QI'E JINGDIAN · MINGREN DA FAXIAN：ZHONG-YING SHUANGYU BAN HALI HUDINI
企鹅经典 · 名人大发现：中英双语版　哈里 · 胡迪尼

著　　者：［美］图伊 · T. 萨瑟兰（Tui T. Sutherland）
绘　　者：［美］约翰 · 奥布赖恩（John O'Brien）
译　　者：曹幼南
出 版 人：潘晓山
责任编辑：刘　竞
策划出品：李　炜　张苗苗　文赛峰
策划编辑：马　瑄
特约编辑：杜佳美
营销编辑：付　佳　杨　朔　周晓茜
装帧设计：利　锐
内文排版：金锋工作室
出　　版：湖南科学技术出版社
（湖南省长沙市芙蓉中路416号　邮编：410008）
网　　址：www.hnstp.com
印　　刷：三河市航远印刷有限公司
经　　销：新华书店
开　　本：875 mm × 1230 mm 1/32
字　　数：105千字
印　　张：6
版　　次：2025年1月第1版
印　　次：2025年1月第1次印刷
书　　号：ISBN 978-7-5710-3268-5
定　　价：22.00元

若有质量问题，请致电质量监督电话：010-59096394　　团购电话：010-59320018

目 录

Contents

谁是哈里·胡迪尼？

大多数人都知道他是著名的魔术师，但你知道吗？他也是电影明星、飞行员、杂技演员和作家。

哈里·胡迪尼实际上并不喜欢“魔术师”这个词，他更喜欢把自己称为“逃脱艺术家”。他说任何东西都困不住他，手铐、牢房、约束衣、铁链、上了锁的箱子、铁笼子等通通不行。于是人们向胡迪尼发起挑战，用千奇百怪的锁把他锁在五花八门的地方，但他总是能成功逃脱！

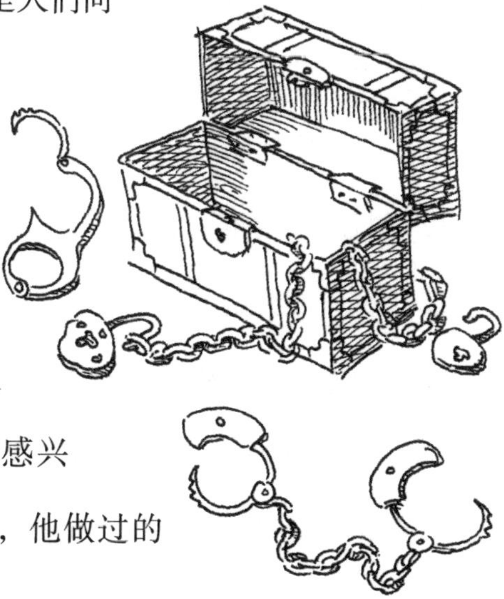

为什么直到今天人们仍对哈里·胡迪尼很感兴趣呢？其中一个原因是，他做过的

很多事情别人未曾做到，他的许多魔术在今天仍是个谜。他讲述过很多自己人生的传奇故事，但我们有时难以判断那些故事的真假。我们也不知道他为什么会去做那些疯狂而又危险的事情。是为了惊艳他人吗？是因为他认为那会给他带来大笔财富？还是因为他想在某方面成为世界首屈一指的人物，并且想让全世界都知道这一点呢？哈里·胡迪尼无疑是一位天赋异禀的逃脱艺术家。更重要的是，胡迪尼有着坚韧不拔的品格，他想要的，他就要得到。胡迪尼想要的是人们的关注——大量的关注！

在那个还没有电视和电影的时代，哈里·胡迪尼成了举世闻名的人，几乎每个人都知道他是谁。他努力做到了这一点。在当今社会，你能想象出不依靠电视、电脑或电影就能出名的人吗？

出名对胡迪尼来说非常重要，他也最终实现了这一梦想。即使到了今天，在他去世七十五年之后，他仍然是最著名的魔术师。

第一章

成为美国人

1886年，一个十二岁的男孩站在一处火车站的站台上。他个子不高，但是肌肉发达，面容刚毅，长着一头乌黑的头发，一双蓝灰色的眼睛明亮有神。此时他正皱着眉头。

这根本不是他要去的地方。

他在北边距离此地几百英里[①]远的威斯康星州密尔沃基市跳上了一列火车。他认为该火车开往得克萨斯州，那正是他打算去的地方。半路上，他还给母亲寄了一张明信片。

① 英里：英美制长度单位。1 英里 = 5280 英尺 ≈ 1.6093 千米。

但是，这里并不是得克萨斯州，因为站台上的标牌明明白白地写着“密苏里州堪萨斯城”。不知怎的，他上错了火车，此刻到的这个地方，距离得克萨斯州有几百英里远。

他能怎么办呢？

只能尽力而为了。毕竟，他为了给家里挣钱，已经从家里跑出来了。他之前的打算是找些给人跑腿、擦鞋的活计做，能找到什么活计就干什么活计。他既然能在得克萨斯州找事情做，当然也能在密苏里州找事情做。于是他向着城区走去，去找个睡觉的地方。

在后来的岁月里，这个男孩到过比密苏里州堪萨斯城还要远的地方。他最初只是打算挣一些面额五分、一角的硬币回家，从没想到会有挣到成百上千美元的那一天。那时的那个年轻的擦鞋童怎么也不会想到，他有朝一日会成为举世闻名的魔术师。他当时可连挣口饭吃都

成问题！

哈里·胡迪尼的童年充满了各种离奇故事，这些故事可能是真的，也可能是假的。他于1874年3月24日出生在匈牙利的布达佩斯，真名叫埃里克·魏斯，但他在世时，总是说自己的生日是4月6日，因为他母亲就是这么告诉他的。有时，他也会说自己出生在美国。他的回答取决于他面对的记者是谁！

那时，许多欧洲人认为美国是个神奇的地方，到了美国，他们所有的问题都会迎刃而解。成千上万的人从欧洲来到美国，希望开启新的人生起点，也希望赚很多钱。哈里的父亲就是其中之一。

哈里的父亲名叫迈尔·沙穆埃尔·魏斯，是一位犹太教拉比。在匈牙利，犹太人生存艰难，因为这个国家在法律上把犹太人当成二等公民，人们也看不起犹太人，犹太人很难找到工作。魏斯家很穷。沙穆埃尔觉得也许他去了美国情况会好些，毕竟人们把那里称为“机会之国”。因此 1876 年，也就是埃里克两岁的那年，沙穆埃尔离开了妻子和儿子。虽然他一句英语也不会说，但他还是启程前往大洋彼岸的美国。他花了两年时间才攒够钱，把家人也接到美国。

你能想象得出他们去美国的旅程是什么样的吗？首先，哈里的母亲塞西莉亚和她的四个儿子必须从匈牙利赶往一个港口城市。从那里，他们将登上一艘前往美国的轮船，和他们一同登船的还有其他多达两千人的

自由女神像

1886 年，法国送给美国的礼物，庆祝美国建国一百周年。

旅客。像这样的大船横渡大西洋需要两周到两个月的时间，乘客们必须忍受着拥挤的环境和有限的食物供给。因此，胡迪尼终其一生都讨厌乘船旅行。

今天，自由女神像矗立在纽约的港口，欢迎着新移民的到来。但埃里克和家人抵达时，自由女神像还没有建成。美国是一个巨大、陌生而又全新的世界，现在这里成了埃里克的新家。

不幸的是，在美国的生活并不轻松多少。魏斯夫妇从纽约搬到威斯康星州，先是住在一座叫阿普尔顿的小城里，后来又搬到了密尔沃基市。埃里克年仅八岁时就开始工作，帮助家里挣钱支付账单。他卖过报纸，擦过皮鞋，帮人跑过腿。九岁时，他还在一个后院马戏团里表演了他的第一个明星节目，该

马戏团是他和朋友们一起组建的。他自封为"空中王子"，在树上自制了一个高空秋千架，他在上面进行特技表演。后来，关于这段时期的生活，他向记者编造了一些故事。他要么说他小时候参加过真正的巡回马戏团，要么说他在九岁时就已经开始了他那著名的逃脱术表演！事实上，那时他对魔术并不真的感兴趣，但他却喜欢杂技表演——以及掌声。

关于埃里克离家出走的经历，人们知之甚少，只知道他在十二岁时曾离家出走过一段时间。他离家出走可能不止一次，尽管他非常爱自己的家人。他总是计划着挣到了钱就回家。

埃里克因这些独自生活与旅行的经历变得聪明机敏。因此，当沙穆埃尔在 1887 年搬到纽约，希望在那里能有更好的运气时，他选择了将十三岁的埃里克（尽管不是长子）带在身边。父子俩一起努力，终于筹到了足够的钱，让家里的其他人也搬到了纽约。

沙穆埃尔·魏斯于 1892 年去世，留下了妻子和六个孩子无人照料。不过，埃里克坚信自己能解决家里面临的困难。对他的父亲来说，美国从来都不是机会之国，但是埃里克下定决心，一定要让美国成为自己的机会之国。

他父亲临终让埃里克答应他一件事：永远照顾好他的母亲。埃里克是守诺之人，对这个承诺更是重视。塞西莉亚·魏斯在之后的人生中，总是能依靠她这个“逃学的儿子”。

有一个关于他童年的故事，哈里·胡迪尼在晚年时总是喜欢说起。不管是不是真的，这个故事听起来确实像他的风格。故事发生在 12 月里的一天，当时埃里克在做信差，他突然想到了一个好主意。他写好一张卡片，将其贴到了帽子上。

卡片上写着：

圣诞来，火鸡肥，请往信差的帽子里投一枚

二十五美分的硬币吧。

许多人看到后，都笑着给了他硬币。那天晚上，他回到家里，把所有的硬币都藏到他的头发和衣服里，然后走到妈妈跟前说：“摇一摇我！我会法术！”于是她就照着他的话做了，硬币飞了出来，滚得满地都是——就像被施了魔法一样！

在他十六岁左右的时候，埃里克读到一本书，名为《罗贝尔–乌丹回忆录》。这是19世纪法国一位著名魔术师的自传，书中充满了奇幻故事，埃里克被深深地吸引住了。

如果罗贝尔-乌丹能依靠魔术出名，那埃里克·魏斯也可以！但他需要取一个更加引人注意的舞台艺名。他的家人叫他“埃里”，听起来像哈里。法语名字“Houdin”（乌丹）能让人联想到魔术，哈里再在后面加个字母i，变成了“Houdini”，而“Houdini”在英语中的发音类似“胡迪尼”，于是哈里·胡迪尼这个名字便诞生了。

罗贝尔－乌丹

在让－欧仁·罗贝尔－乌丹（1805—1871年）之前，魔术表演都在露天市场或街角进行。罗贝尔－乌丹能够变出前人未曾想到的魔术，将魔术变成了一门艺术。他在魔术中运用了科学

发展的新成果。（他最初只是一个钟表匠！）与哈里·胡迪尼一样，罗贝尔－乌丹的思想也非常现代。他研究电磁学，因此他会使用强力磁铁将舞台上的物体移来移去。

罗贝尔－乌丹还非常善于宣传自己。他的自传（1857 年出版）里满是离奇和荒诞的故事。然而，他的魔术技艺和风格十分成功，以至于时至今日，罗贝尔－乌丹仍被认为是“现代魔术之父”。

第二章

成为魔术师

对哈里来说，成功并不像“变魔术一样”突然降临。一个人到底要如何做才能成为一名魔术师呢？这与成为医生或律师不同，因为没有专门的魔术师学校。哈里经过了多年努力才成为魔术师。

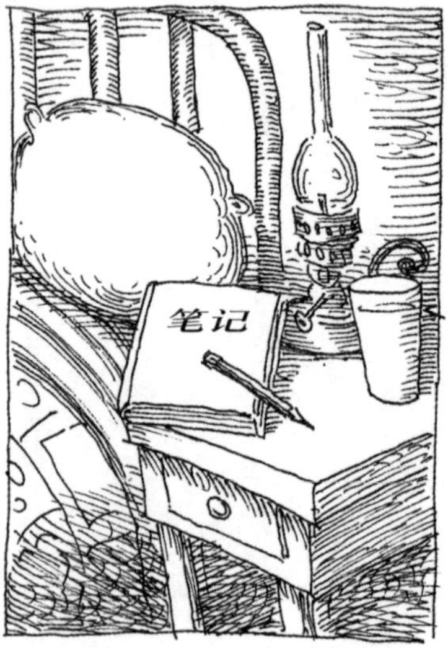

首先，魔术师必须学会很多魔术技法。即使成名之后，哈里也一直在寻找新的技法和幻术。他观看其他魔术师的表演，阅读有关魔术的书籍，把一切记在笔记本上。他的床边总是放着一本笔记本，以备半夜想到什么。

要成为一名魔术师还需要不断地练习。哈里反复练习他的魔术技法。他做特殊的练习，以保持手脚灵活敏捷。他随身携带一枚硬币，每当他没表演时，就用手指快速翻动硬币。你可以试一试，做起来可比看上去要难！

消失的硬币

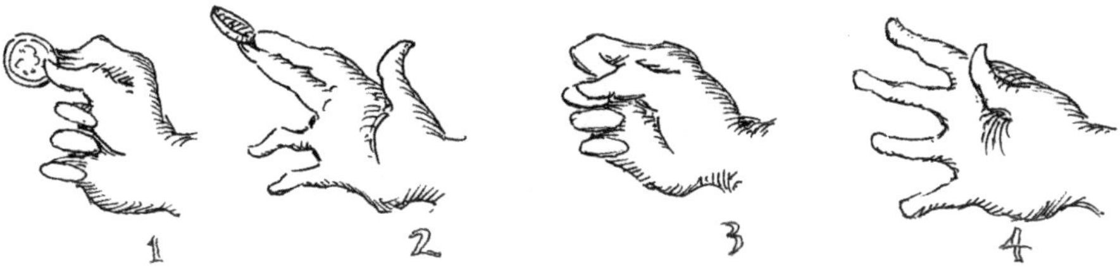

除了学习和练习，哈里还必须努力推销自己。即使最好的魔术师也需要观众，哈里必须想办法吸引人们来看他的表演。他必须引起人们的关注。

哈里最初的魔术表演叫“胡迪尼兄弟”。他的弟弟西奥当他的搭档，他们一起表演纸牌魔术、读心术、消失魔术和幻术。

幻术是创造一种看似发生了，但逻辑上不可能发生的事情。举个例子，你见过魔术师从别人耳朵里掏出一枚硬币吗？这就是幻术。或者魔术师把一张纸撕成碎片，然后奇迹出现了！它又恢复成了一张完整的纸。从逻辑上讲，纸是不可能自己恢复原样的，魔术师也不可能在别人的耳朵里找到硬币。但是魔术完成得非常快，观众看着就像真的一样。

哈里和西奥经常表演这类魔术，他们在任何能表演的地方表演。他们总是会把部分钱存下来，寄给家里的母亲。最让他们兴奋的表演之一是 1893 年在芝加哥世界博览会上的杂耍表演。当时哈里只有十九岁，西奥十七岁。

西奥和哈里相处融洽。西奥在某些方面和哈里很像——他也喜欢魔术（后来他也成了一名魔术师）。但是，他们之间也存在着矛盾。一天晚上，西奥搞砸了他们最拿手的魔术。哈里讨厌失误，他认为在观众面前就应该一切完美无瑕，但是西奥就是跟不上他的节奏。哈里需要一个能替代西奥的人。很快，这个人出现了。

1894 年夏天，胡迪尼兄弟与一个叫“花样姐妹”的歌舞表演组合在同一个小镇演出。姐妹中的一人是个身材娇小的棕发女孩，名叫比阿特丽斯·雷蒙德。和哈里一样，她也为登台表演取了艺名。她的真名叫威廉明娜·拉纳，但大家都叫她贝丝。她当时十八岁，而哈里二十岁。

贝丝和哈里一见钟情。有些故事说他俩相识仅两周就结婚了。根据其中一个故事的说法，贝丝不得不偷偷溜出家门与哈里约会，因为她担心母亲知道了会发怒。当天晚上，贝丝告诉哈里她害怕回家，于是他当场向她求婚，两人当晚就结婚了！即便这不是真的，但可以肯定的是他们相爱了，并且很快就结了婚。贝丝的母亲对此不满也是事实，因为贝丝来自天主教家庭，而哈里是犹太人，是犹太教拉比的儿子。但是，哈里的母亲并不介意，她觉得贝丝很好。哈里也这样认为。

贝丝不仅是个完美的妻子，也是理想的舞台搭档。她已经熟悉了舞台表演，很乐意在哈里魔术表演的间隙唱歌跳舞，而且总是能很有风度地为哈里报幕。她还很

快学会了那些魔术，因此可以协助哈里完成所有的表演。

贝丝个子娇小，只有五英尺[①]高！这让哈里看起来高大伟岸，实际上他只有五英尺五英寸（约 165 厘米）或五英尺六英寸（约 168 厘米）高。这种身型还意味着她可以在狭小的地方顺利进出，这对逃脱术表演很有利。

即使哈里在后来进行个人表演时，贝丝也一直陪着他四处旅行。她负责他的日程安排，记录他的演出过程，提醒他每天都记得换衬衫。哈里说他能出名全是她的功

① 1 英尺 = 12 英寸，1 英寸 = 2.54 厘米，5 英尺约等于 152 厘米。

劳："她给我带来了好运，从那时起，好运就一直伴随我左右。娶她之前，我可从未有过如此好运。"直到哈里去世，他和贝丝都一直在一起。

19 世纪 90 年代，哈里在贝丝的帮助下在被称为"一角钱博物馆[①]"的大礼堂里表演，人们只需花十美分就能进去观看一些稀奇古怪的表演，如吞剑、耍猴、杂耍等。胡迪尼表演的是"变形"魔术。

胡迪尼个子不高，穿着破旧的燕尾服，一脸严肃地站在一个箱子上，向人群挥手致意。贝丝和他站在一起，身穿紧身羊毛裤和宽松的白色上衣。

首先，哈里会从观众中挑选出几个人来组成一个"委员会"，然后让他们来检查"设备"。设备是一个高高的柜子，里面有一只箱子。箱子大小可以容纳一个人。委员会必须查看箱子。他们敲遍箱子的每一个面，看了

---

① 一角钱博物馆（Dime Museum），意同其名，指便宜的博物馆，流行于 19 世纪后期的美国。它被视为供下层民众娱乐消遣和进行道德教育的中心，活动项目包括杂耍表演、畸形秀等。

箱子的里面。最后，他们会宣布箱子看起来一切正常，不存在暗门之类的东西。

接下来，哈里递给委员会一个黑色的大袋子和一些厚胶带。他们按照哈里的要求，把他的双手绑在一起，协助他钻入袋子里，然后用胶带把袋子封得严严实实。接着，他们把装着哈里的袋子放进箱子里，锁上箱子，用粗绳子绑紧，再把箱子放进柜子里。

一切就绪后，贝丝拉上柜子前的幕布。

“现在，女士们，先生们，”贝丝说，戏剧性地停顿了一下，“我将拍三次手，在拍最后一次时，我请你们……仔细观察……”她一边拍手，一边走到幕布后面。不到三秒钟，幕布拉开了。站在观众面前的是谁呢？哈里·胡迪尼！贝丝去哪里了呢？

哈里转过身，看向箱子，箱子仍然是封着的。在委员会的帮助下，他解下绳子并打开箱子上的锁，箱子里的袋子露了出来。他们打开袋子，里面的人居然是贝丝！她和哈里之前一样被绑着！

变形魔术

变形魔术委员会检查设备

他钻进箱子里的袋子里，委员会将他的双手绑起来，并系上袋口。

用粗绳子绑好箱子，并用粗链子锁上，然后将箱子放入柜子。

贝丝拉上柜子前的幕布，和观众说话，拍三次手，然后走到幕布后。

幕布拉开时，哈里站在箱子旁。

然后他打开箱子和袋子，里面出现的是贝丝。

怎么做到的？

哈里解开手上的绳子，用藏起来的小刀把袋子底部割开，接着通过箱子后面的一块滑动的木板爬出来。然后，贝丝通过滑动的木板爬进袋子，取代哈里的位置。

这和西奥之前搞砸的魔术如出一辙，但是贝丝身型更小，而且手脚更快，可以如哈里希望的那样瞬间完成魔术。她变化——或“变形”——的速度很快，看起来就像真的有魔力在起作用。

第三章

出名

变形魔术是令人惊叹的幻术表演，但还不足以让“胡迪尼夫妇”的名气像哈里希望的那样大，表演需要添加戏剧性的新元素。

哈里尝试了不同类型的节目。他和贝丝一起表演过读心术、马戏杂技，甚至好几次假装“和死人说话”。他怎么能和死人说话呢？是依靠他的聪明才智，再加上调查研究实现的。他们每到一个新的城镇，哈里会阅读当地的报纸，会去墓地看一看谁刚死不久，会听一听人们讲述他们朋友的故事。然后，在舞台上他会利用这些信息让人们以为他真的在和鬼魂说话。观众对此深信不疑。不过，胡迪尼只表演了几次就放弃了“与死人说话”这个节目。他不喜欢以这种方式骗人。这与魔术不同，因为观众知道魔术必定使用了障眼法或技巧。

幸运的是，哈里最终找到了让他闻名世界的独特节目：逃脱术表演。在胡迪尼之前，其他魔术师也曾在表演中使用手铐，但他是第一个将手铐作为表演主要看点之人，也是第一个当着观众的面，尝试从约束衣中逃脱之人。

约束衣是一种有带子和锁扣，结构复杂的外套。它们用于防止有暴力倾向的人伤害自己或他人。穿约束衣的人胳膊和手根本使不上力。哈里认为他可以从约束衣的束缚中逃脱。经过反复练习和努力，他真的可以做到这一点。这个节目在舞台上的表演效果非常好，令观众

前面

后面

从约束衣中逃脱的过程

1. 收紧约束衣时，尽量扩展胸膛与肩膀。

2. 紧缩胸膛和肩膀，然后将手臂抬起，举过头顶。

3. 手臂松开后，就可以解开约束衣后背上的锁扣，最后身体获得自由。

印象深刻。他决定不躲在幕布后表演，因为这根本不是什么戏法，只是需要许多技巧和努力（以及练习）。观众即使看完了他的表演，也无法解释他是如何做到的。当然，也没有其他人能够做到！

哈里还想出了别出心裁的方法来宣传他的表演。每当他和贝丝新到一个城镇，他会直接去当地的警察局。

“我是哈里·胡迪尼，手铐之王！”他对警察说，“把我绑上，关起来，用你们的手铐把我铐上。我向你们保证我能立刻逃脱。”

这样做通常会招致警察们的嘲笑。这个说大话的矮子以为自己是谁？他们可从来没听说过什么“哈里·胡迪尼”。所有人都以为魔术师们使用的都是动了手脚的手铐，没有人能从真正的手铐中逃脱。对这一点，他们十分肯定，于是让哈里把当地报社的记者邀来观看。警察会搜查哈里的全身，以防他带着工具（有时他们甚至坚持让他光着身子表演，这样就能确定他没有在衣服里藏匿钥匙）。接着，他们会把他捆绑起来，在他的手脚上扣上几副手铐，然后把他关进一个房间里，或把他锁进一间牢房里。

“过一会儿，我们会来放你出去。”警察开玩笑说。之后，他们便坐到隔壁房间议论起这个爱过分卖弄的人。令他们吃惊的是，几分钟后，哈里走进他们的房间，手

里还举着手铐。有时，他不到一分钟就能逃出来。

警察和新闻记者们都大为震惊。他们不知道他是如何做到的。哈里没有因为这些特技表演而得到任何报酬，但这并不重要，因为报纸对他的表演进行了大量报道，引起了人们的关注，吸引他们前来观看他的演出。他们想亲眼看一看这个能骗过当地警察的魔术师。

问题是，一次特技表演只对一个城镇有效。他可以在密苏里州的某个小城这样做，并在一个晚上就在当地声名大噪。但要是去了另一个地方，他就又成了无名小卒，一切又得从头开始。注意，那时没有电视和互联网，很难把新闻传遍全国，尤其这新闻还只是关于一个小小

的魔术表演。

到了1899年，哈里和贝丝已经一起到处演出了整整五年时间。哈里变得有些灰心丧气。他开始想要出售他的魔术秘诀，甚至想过完全放弃魔术事业，退出魔术界。然而，在紧要关头，哈里得到了别人的赏识。

一天晚上，有个人来看胡迪尼的表演。他对胡迪尼说：“嘿，你的表演真不赖。这样吧，别表演纸牌魔术和撕纸幻术了，只表演二十分钟的逃脱术，包括‘变形魔术’，我一定能让你一举成名。”

这个人是谁呢？他是马丁·贝克，是著名的奥芬剧院的负责人。奥芬剧院是一家全国性连锁剧院，或者说是“歌舞杂耍戏院”。

歌舞杂耍戏院比一角钱博物馆高级多了，每晚都有不同的表演者演出：歌手、舞者、杂技演员、喜剧演员等等。马丁认为哈里的表演非常适合杂耍戏院，因为他的表演新颖、刺激、与众不同。他认为哈里有可能取得巨大成功。当然，哈里自己也一直这么认为。

他们的想法是对的。几乎一夜间，哈里成了轰动一时的人物。他终于有时间专注于自己最擅长的领域——逃脱术。1899 年底，他每周能赚到一百多美元，这在当时可是笔不小的收入。最重要的是，他得到了梦寐以求的公众关注。

现在，哈里为走向世界做好了准备，同时，世界也为接纳他做好了准备。

第四章

成为明星

十四个月后，对哈里来说，奥芬剧院的舞台显得有些小了，仅在美国成功还远远不够。想要成为真正的明星，哈里·胡迪尼必须征服欧洲。

1900年5月，在移民到美国二十二年后，哈里再次穿越大西洋，但这一次与上一次的方向相反，和他同行的有贝丝和他们的狗查理。这次旅行仍然是一次漫长的旅行（快船也需要两周）。哈里全程晕船晕得很厉害，但这并没有阻止他为其他乘客表演纸牌魔术。

哈里的欧洲巡演之旅从英国开始。当然，哈里和贝丝刚到英国时，还没有人听说过哈里·胡迪尼。他不得不重新开始推销自己。但这一次，他没费多少时间。这个“手铐之王”从伦敦警察厅的手铐中成功逃脱，令伦敦最高级别的警察困惑不解。胡迪尼凭着这一壮举进入了伦敦最高级别的剧院——阿罕布拉剧院。

阿罕布拉剧院是哈里演出过的所有剧院中最为出色的。它看起来更像歌剧院，而不像歌舞杂耍戏院。观众们也更加文雅和矜持。在美国，哈里曾因语法错误和服装寒酸而受到一些人的差评。到了这里，他每晚登台亮相时都穿着正式燕尾服，打着白色领结。他对自己的语言进行打磨润色，使其在能吸引观众的同时，听起来更加高贵庄重。他反复练习，不断思考如何在表演中加入新的技法。

所有这一切都奏效了，观众喜欢上了胡迪尼。整个 7 月和 8 月，哈里都在阿罕布拉剧院演出，圣诞节时他又回到了这里表演。哈里最初的计划是在欧洲表演几场，然后就返回美国。结果，哈里和贝丝在欧洲一待就是五年。

胡迪尼夫妇到过欧洲许多国家演出。每到一个地方，哈里都会努力学习当地的语言，以便在演出时能用当地语言和观众交流。这一点在德国最容易做到，因为他从小就和父母说德语。他深受德国观众喜爱，在德国获得了巨大成功。不过，在德国表演也有危险，因为德国警方有时会以“欺骗民众”的罪名逮捕艺人，艺人演出必须得到警方的批准。

胡迪尼不得不在三百个警察面前“试演”。他们提供了所有的锁，并事先搜查了哈里全身，防止他携带钥匙。为了保护他的魔术秘密，他们同意他盖着毯子表演。当然，他轻易就逃脱了，仅用了六分钟！由于警方无法解释他是如何做到的，因此他们不得不让他继续演出。

哈里最严峻的考验发生在英国一个叫布莱克本的城市。当时，哈里提出，谁要是能提供他无法逃脱的手铐，他愿意支付二十五英镑，这可是一大笔钱。1902 年 10 月 24 日，哈里的表演进行到一半时，有个人突然走上舞台。他的名字叫威廉·霍奇森，他想和哈里打赌。哈里立刻对霍奇森的手铐产生了怀疑。手铐看起来已经损坏，甚至可能已经断裂，这会让其很难打开。但霍奇森取笑道，胡迪尼害怕接受真正的挑战。哈里·胡迪尼绝对不能容忍别人这么说他。

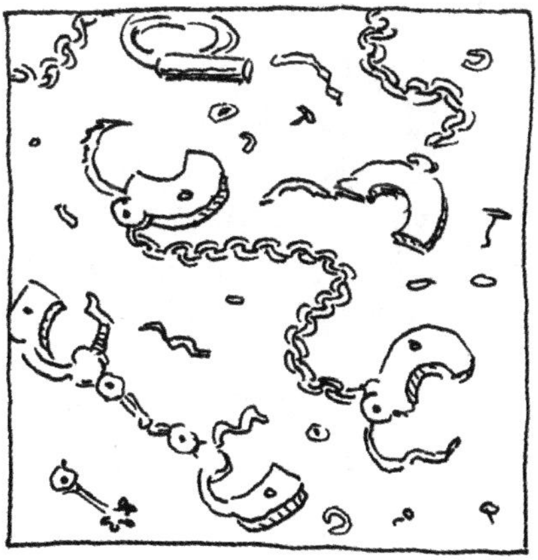

霍奇森是一个体能专家，他仔细研究过人体和所有肌肉工作的原理。他清楚地知道应该如何绑人才会让这个人完全无法动弹。他以这种方式将胡迪尼绑了起来，用上了铁链和六副手铐。围观的人不是担心哈里的血液

循环会被完全阻断，就是担心霍奇森的动作过于粗暴，会扭断哈里的手臂。但对哈里来说，难度最大的地方是他的逃脱技法取决于他的力量和身体的灵活性。如果他不能动弹，这些技法就发挥不了作用。

胡迪尼在幕后拼命挣扎，惊恐的观众等了足足一个半小时。哈里曾一度要求将他的手腕松开片刻，因为他的双手已经麻了，完全没有了知觉。霍奇森拒绝了哈里的要求。他说："如果你认输，就放弃吧。"哈里·胡迪尼是不可能认输的！他又回到了幕后。

午夜刚过，幕布突然被拉开。哈里站在台上，得意扬扬地将最后一副手铐扔在了舞台上。一个记者后来说，哈里看上去"就像被老虎爪子挠过一样"，全身都是血痕和

瘀青，但他挣脱了所有的束缚。全场为之轰动。

他在英国还有另一件事成了头条新闻。一份名为《伦敦每日镜报》的报纸挑战胡迪尼，请他尝试一副“史上最难逃脱的手铐”。这样的挑战，哈里如何能拒绝呢？

人们称这副手铐为“镜报手铐”，是由英国伯明翰的一个人制作出来的。此人声称这副手铐花了五年时间才制作完成。胡迪尼在多年研究制锁工艺的过程中了解到，大多数锁的机械构造都很简单，只需几把简单的钥匙就能打开，有的甚至只需要在正确的地方轻轻一敲，就能打开。但这副手铐却比普通手铐复杂上千倍，这世上只有一把钥匙能将其打开，而这把钥匙在制作此锁的锁匠手里。

演出前几天，报纸上报道了有关“镜报手铐”和向胡迪尼发起的挑战。这正中哈里下怀，对他来说，关注越多越好。那个重要的夜晚终于来临，哈里出现在舞台上，全场起立鼓掌欢迎。像往常一样，他从观众中选出了一个委员会来确保表演过程公平公正。《伦敦每日镜报》记者将手铐扣在哈里的手腕上，接着锁匠转动了钥匙六次。

哈里对观众说：“这副手铐是一个英国锁匠花了五年时间才制作出来的。现在，我戴上了这副手铐，我不知道自己能否逃脱，但我向大家保证，我定会尽力而为。”

然后，哈里消失在了舞台的幕布后。接下来的很长一段时间里，观众们只能看见时不时动一下的幕布。

这是哈里表演的另一个有趣之处。他的大部分表演都在幕布后进行，其间，观众一直等待结果。想象一下，如果当今的人们去看演出，他们大部分时间都只是盯着幕布，情况会怎么样呢？那时的观众可有耐心多了，而且哈里在舞台上魅力非凡，光彩夺目，即使他出场也就那么几分钟，观众也觉得花时间看整场演出是值得的。此外，他们总是带着一个疑问：他能成功逃脱吗？还是会失败呢？

戴上“镜报手铐”几分钟后，哈里从幕布后走了出来，看上去已经筋疲力尽了。他逃脱了吗？没有！他只是想找个垫子，方便跪在上面，之后他就回幕布后了。

不久，他又走了出来，但是等等——他还戴着手铐！这一次，他要求打开手铐片刻，以便脱掉外套。《伦敦每日镜报》的代表说不行。如果让哈里看见手铐打开的过程，他可能会获得解开手铐的线索。手铐必须得一直戴着，直到哈里认输为止。

认输？哈里·胡迪尼从不认输！他站在台上，借助牙齿帮忙，并扭转手臂，成功地从上衣口袋里拿出一把小刀。他出人意料地将外套翻过头顶，用牙齿咬住小刀，使劲划着大衣，直到大衣被划成碎片，散落到地上。他神气地甩了甩头，转身再次消失在幕布后。

仅仅过了十分钟，哈里就一跃而出，手里高举“镜报手铐”。他成功了，“手铐之王”胜利了！人群沸腾起来。这件事在报纸上连着刊登了好些天。制作这副手铐花了五年时间，而胡迪尼仅用了一小时就成功破解了它。

哈里在欧洲还有许多不寻常的经历。在巴黎时，他曾为他的英雄让－欧仁·罗贝尔－乌丹扫墓。事实上，他去过很多著名魔术师的墓地，给他们送去大花圈。他还拜访了许多知名的退休魔术师，其中一些人被他的成功和魅力所折服，甚至和他分享了自己的魔术秘诀。

哈里去过的所有国家中，最不欢迎他的也许是俄罗斯。作为一个犹太人，他不能用自己的护照入境俄罗斯。胡迪尼夫妇不得不使用贝丝的护照和证件，因为她是罗马天主教徒。

这也让他更清楚地认识到有多少人憎恨犹太人。这种偏见和反犹太主义的思想正是他和家人多年前离开欧洲的重要原因。

不过，哈里大多数时候还是十分喜欢欧洲的。即使在一个城市待上几个月，他的演出仍然每晚座无虚席。而在美国，他每隔一周左右就要去一个新的地方。他在欧洲赚到的钱也多得惊人。尽管如此，哈里还是非常想念他的母亲。他经常给母亲寄钱，并在1900年至1905年间探望母亲两次。但他还是想离母亲更近一些，也不想美国忘记他，于是，1905 年，美国迎来了国际巨星哈里 · 胡迪尼的回归。

第五章

成为世人惊叹的逃脱大师

从那时起，哈里 · 胡迪尼的脚步就未曾停歇。他的足迹遍布美国乃至全世界。他向世人发起挑战，鼓励人们寻找他无法逃脱的东西并把他锁在里面。他逃脱过的东西千奇百怪，其中有一个是巨大的足球！他还为自己的表演添加了一个新元素——水。

1908 年，胡迪尼首次表演了一个全新的魔术，他曾称其为“我发明的最佳魔术”！这个魔术让剧院里的观众坐立不安。哈里一开始表演的是他的一些标准节目——幻术、变形魔术、手铐逃脱术。接着，他转身向台下的观众走去。他跨过舞台底部的脚灯，身体前倾，仿佛要跃向第一排座位，张开双臂。

“女士们，先生们！”哈里说，他的声音低沉有力，清楚地传到了后排。他不再是那个在一角钱博物馆表演时，衣着寒酸、沉默寡言的男孩了。他此时魅力十足，点燃了全场观众的热情。“今天，我生平第一次向大家介绍这场最新、最伟大的逃脱术表演，这也是美国舞台上有史以来最精彩的表演！”

哈里大手一挥，观众眼前出现了一个巨大的铁质牛奶罐，体积庞大，足够容纳一个小个子的人挤进去。他把罐子四周锤得砰砰直响，以此告诉大家它有多结实。然后，他走到台下换上泳衣，他的助手则把罐子灌满水。

最后，哈里爬进了罐子。“当我沉入水里时，”他对观众说，“你们自己也试着计一计时，看看自己憋气能憋多久。”他还指了指他的一个助手，那人手里拿着一把大斧头。“万一出了问题，不要害怕。我忠实的助手会砸开罐子，把我解救出来……但愿那时还来得及！”

胡迪尼面带微笑，任凭别人给自己扣上手铐，然后挤进了罐子里。他的助手们用好几把巨大的挂锁锁住了钢铁盖子。在后来的表演版本中，哈里还会邀请观众带上他们自己的挂锁，以便把盖子锁得更加牢固。

幕布被拉上，挡住了罐子。观众们屏住呼吸。时间一秒一秒地过去，整整一分钟过去了。此时，大多数观众都在大口喘气。憋那么久的气是非常危险的，但还是没有人看到胡迪尼的踪影。两分钟过去了，三分钟过去了，观众们焦急起来。胡迪尼要是淹死了怎么办？罐子外的人又怎么知道呢？“放他出来！”他们开始大喊，“砸开罐子！他快淹死了！”

突然，哈里一把拉开幕布，朝着观众鞠了一躬。他浑身湿漉漉的，大口喘着粗气，但是他还活着，并已获得自由。罐子还在原处，上面的挂锁仍然好好地锁着。

这真是惊险刺激的魔术表演，观众们欲罢不能，百看不厌。哈里也喜欢操控人们的心理，让逃脱过程看起来更加富有戏剧性。有时，他几分钟就能从罐子里出来，然后在幕布后等上半个小时，让紧张气氛不断升温。一旦所有人都惊恐地认为表演失败了，胡迪尼死

了，他就会戏剧性地现身，引起全场雷鸣般的掌声。

哈里一直是游泳健将，在水中游刃有余。为了完成这个极度危险的表演，他进行了大量练习。他会在浴缸里装满水，让贝丝给他计时，看自己能在水里待多久。有时他会把水温调得很低，看自己能忍耐多久。这么做对他的另一个更加危险的新节目——河中逃生——也很有帮助。

哈里通常会在一座桥上开始这个节目的表演，周围有成千上万的观众（当然还有记者）！他会脱去身上的衣物，脱得只剩下泳衣或长内衣裤，接着让警察用两副或两副以上的手铐锁住他。之后，他爬上栏杆，挥挥手，向人群大声道别，然后纵身一跃，跳下大桥，落入冰凉彻骨的河水中。水花四溅！观众们俯身在栏杆上，目光搜索着水面。有时，胡迪尼会马上探出头来，得意扬扬地把手铐举过头顶。有时他会在水下滞留更长的时间，让大家焦心等待。有几次，他甚至从水下潜到某个可以藏身的地方躲起来。

哈里总是强调这是他最危险的逃脱术表演。他警告别人不要去尝试，但总有些人会去尝试，其中一些因此而死。水非常冷，很危险，而且，水流有时还会把胡迪尼从等着救他的助手所在的船只边冲走。有一次，他被困在了冰面下，因为水流把他冲离了他计划跳出的冰面洞口。

胡迪尼不断为他的水下逃生表演设计新的、更危险的花样。有时他会在手铐上绑上又大又重的东西，加快他沉底的速度。有时，他除了让人绑着，还会被装进木箱子里，箱子被钉上后再被扔进河里。

他在美国各个城市表演跳桥逃生，从纽约州的罗切斯特到马萨诸塞州的波士顿，再到路易斯安那州的新奥尔良。这种高危特技表演是无法收费的，但哈里并不介意，就像他之前挑战警察一样，他为由此获得的名声和关注感到兴奋。到了此时，他为自己做广告并不难，总会有成千上万的人来观看他的跳桥逃生表演。

胡迪尼最喜欢的就是一大群观众！

第六章

成为飞行员

哈里喜欢出名。他喜欢做到最好，也喜欢争当第一。

飞机是在哈里有生之年被发明出来的。1903 年，莱特兄弟在北卡罗来纳州的基蒂霍克成功试飞了第一架飞机，创造了历史。此时，哈里年近三十。当时的飞机是危险的交通工具，存在很多无法预测的风险，安全性完全赶不上现在的飞机。哈里讨厌乘船，甚至连车都不会开，但当他第一次看到飞机时，他就知道自己必须学会开飞机。不仅如此，他还想在航空史上添上浓墨重彩的一笔。

莱特兄弟的首次飞行只持续了大约十二秒。1909 年，莱特兄弟首次飞行后还不到六年的时间里，有人飞越了英法之间的英吉利海峡；有人进行了第一次夜间飞行；有人实现了第一次载客飞行；有人完成了在法国、

莱特兄弟

威尔伯·莱特
1867—1912

奥维尔·莱特
1871—1948

约五百年前，达·芬奇就曾试图设计出能让人飞行的机器。一直没有人成功做出来，直到1903年12月17日，来自俄亥俄州的莱特兄弟才终于驾驶着他们自己制造的小型飞机飞上了蓝天。

奥维尔·莱特和威尔伯·莱特经营着一家自行车店。安装修理自行车的经验让他们懂得了平衡的重要性，无论是骑车还是驾驶飞机，维持平衡都很重要。他们认识到设计一架飞机需要大量的研究，于是决定自己进行研究和计算。

虽然两人高中都没毕业，但他们还是自学了飞行、风力、物理学等各方面的有用知识。他们还自制了发动机，让发动机的尺寸和重量完全匹配他们的飞机。

最后，在北卡罗来纳州基蒂霍克的那个寒冷的 12 月里的一天，他们的飞机升空了。虽然第一次飞行只持续了十二秒，但它却成了一个历史性的转折点，永远改变了世界。

德国、意大利的第一次飞行。即使是经验丰富的飞行员，也很难再找到新的、能载入史册的飞行事情。哈里仅是个初学者，但他仍然决心成为一个飞行员。于是，他想出了一个计划。

1910 年 1 月，哈里和贝丝登上了一艘巨大的蒸汽船。尽管哈里晕船，但他们还是愿意在船上度过一个多月的时间。是什么原因让他进行这么长时间的远洋航行呢？他们要去哪里呢？

澳大利亚。

澳大利亚距离哈里曾经去过的任何地方都有数千英里之遥。澳大利亚是一个崭新的、仍在发展的大陆。几乎没有一个像他这样大名鼎鼎的表演者愿意长途跋涉到这个南半球的大陆上。但在澳大利亚，还没有人驾驶过飞机。哈里可能在那里成为驾驶飞机第一人。

哈里给自己买了一架叫“瓦赞”的飞机，还雇了一个机械师。他把所有东西都打包好一同带上了蒸汽船。在长达一个月的旅途中，无论哈里晕船晕得多么厉害，他总是想着安全停放在货仓里的飞机。

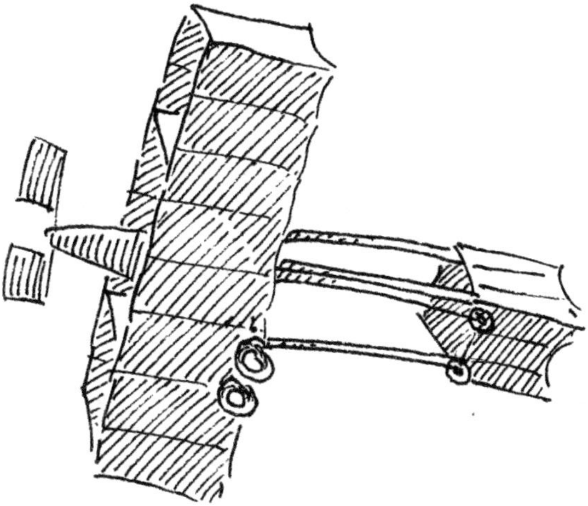

一到澳大利亚，哈里就必须在繁忙的演出日程表中寻找飞行的时间，但时间很难定下来，因为问题层出不穷。那时的飞机很脆弱，所以他不能在大风天、大雾天或大雨天里尝试飞行。等了一个多月，哈里和他的飞机才真正起飞。

1910 年 3 月 18 日上午，在一群记者紧张地注视下，哈里驾驶飞机缓缓绕着场地行驶。哈里在进行了几次短

程试飞，确保一切正常后，将飞机对准场地的另一端。他身体紧绷，全身颤抖，但内心十分坚定。他加速向前，越来越快，最后升空！

官方记录显示，这是在澳大利亚的第一次真正意义上的飞行，飞行持续了大约三分半钟，飞机升到了一百英尺的空中，这足以载入史册。对哈里来说，这就足够了。虽然他后来在澳大利亚又飞了几次，但他逐渐对飞

行失去了兴趣。在与贝丝离开澳大利亚后，他没有再驾驶过飞机。对此，哈里这样解释："我已在空中经历过了。"

几年后，哈里·胡迪尼见到了著名的奥维尔·莱特。结果他发现，奥维尔对哈里飞行经历的了解居然比对胡迪尼魔术的了解还要多。

第七章

成为电影明星

不久，哈里又找到了其他兴趣爱好。20 世纪初，第一批电影在电影院上映。哈里二十一岁时，世界第一部电影在巴黎一家电影院的大银幕上上映。早期的电影是黑白无声电影，由乐队现场演奏音乐。这些电影都很短，动作看起来也不流畅。尽管如此，全世界的人们还是被电影深深吸引。哈里当然不会放过任何一个提升自己名气的机会。还有什么能比拍电影更能提升名气呢？

哈里的第一部影片叫《神秘的大师》，于 1919 年上映，是一部系列电影。这意味着电影是每周分集放映的，而非一次性放映完，这更像电视连续剧而非电影。在系列电影里，每一部的结尾都设置了一个扣人心弦的悬念，例如，女主角被绑在铁轨上，前面是迎面驶来的火车。

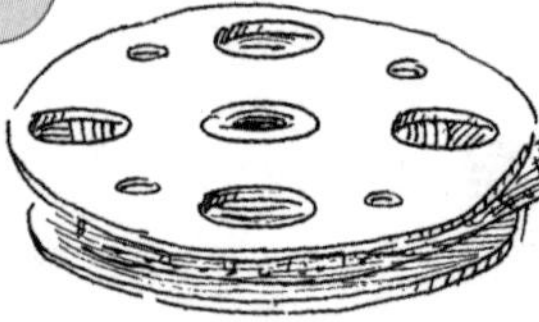

电影

19 世纪末，世界各地的人们都在争先恐后地发明电影摄影机。托马斯·爱迪生发明了一台，之后法国的路易·卢米埃尔发明了一台更好的。卢米埃尔发明的摄影机更加轻巧便携。

路易和哥哥奥古斯特拍摄的第一部电影展现了工厂工人在结束一天工作时的场景。有趣的是，卢米埃尔兄弟认为电影制作没有什么前途！他们想象不出人们为什么要观看那些他们每天都能在现实世界中看到的动态影像。他们根本没想到电影会大受欢迎。

到了 1910 年，无声电影在美国流行起来。第一部系列电影于 1913 年上映。直到 1927 年，也就是胡迪尼去世一年后，才出现有声电影。第一部彩色长篇故事片《浮华世界》于 1935 年上映。

观众必须在下一周来观看另一部，才能知道女主角是否能够死里逃生，以及她是如何逃生的。

这种系列电影几乎就是为哈里·胡迪尼量身打造的。他的整个演艺生涯都在反复陷入看上去不可能逃脱的境地。《神秘的大师》每部的结尾都是哈里陷入可怕的危险中，而下一部就以他成功逃出开始，这样他就可以去追捕“坏人”了。这听起来是不是像一个精彩的电视节目呢？有了电影，此时的观众们可以在银幕上看到胡迪尼著名的逃脱术表演了。

虽然电影尽量避免泄露哈里的逃脱术秘密，但里面还是展示了不少哈里在逃脱过程中需要的技巧和力量。例如，在某个场景中，哈里的双手被锁到墙上，他只好将他那如手指一样灵活的脚趾伸向一串钥匙，挑出正确的钥匙，最后打开牢房的门。

电影的情节非常复杂，而且十分惊险刺激。哈里扮演的是一个政府的卧底人员，而反派则是个机器人。尽管人们看得出机器人里面明显有个人，但这仍然不失为一部电影中的新鲜亮点。《神秘的大师》塑造了电影史上第一个机器人反派角色。

《神秘的大师》在国际上大获成功。印度和日本等地的人们第一次看到了哈里·胡迪尼。当然，多数去看这部电影的人早就知道他这个人了。此时，胡迪尼并不需要借助一部电影来提升他的名气，但他喜欢获得关注，人们也喜欢看他的表演。哈里准备接下来拍摄更多的电影。

在之后的四年里，胡迪尼又主演了四部电影，但影片的收入一部比一部少。《神秘的大师》之后，胡迪尼不再主演系列电影，转而出演长篇故事片。也许，这是观众减少的重要原因——影片不能像以前一样，每周都给观众带来悬念。《残酷游戏》、《惊惧岛》、《来自超越的男人》和《密探霍尔丹》这四部电影得到的评价很糟糕。多数影评人认为：哈里是一位出色的逃脱艺术家，但他根本不会演戏。

然而，最大的问题在于，观众无法分辨出胡迪尼用了真正的逃脱术还是通过摄影技巧创造出了逃脱画面。虽然大部分特技表演都是哈里自己完成的，但电影观众知道在银幕上伪造“危险”实在太容易了。哈里表演的节目性质决定了他在现场的表演更加令人惊心动魄。

不过哈里还是成了电影明星，甚至成了好莱坞星光大道上的一颗耀眼明星。

第八章

成为幻术大师

随着哈里年纪渐长，有些逃脱术节目他表演起来越来越费劲了。他首先放弃了手铐逃脱术表演，反正其他人也在模仿他的这类节目。然后，他开始用非凡的大型幻术表演来取代危险的逃脱术表演。

包括哈里在内的大多数魔术师走上魔术表演之路都是从幻术开始的。从帽子里变兔子就是一个典型的幻术节目。哈里想把幻术提高到一个新的层次，他也的确做到了。

他的一个新幻术节目使用了屏风和一面真正的砖墙。哈里会让一队工人在舞台中央，也就是观众的正前方砌上一堵砖墙。砌之前，舞台的地板上铺着一张大布单，砖墙压在布单上面。哈里会请志愿者上台并站在布单的

砖墙魔术

舞台地板上铺上一块布单，然后在一个带轮子的支架上砌上一面砖墙。

观众志愿者检查墙壁，助理在墙壁两侧放置屏风。

胡迪尼原本在墙壁一侧的屏风后活动，然而却从墙壁另一侧出来。

一个助手打开舞台下面的活板，布单下凹，与砖墙底部形成一个通道，通道大小足够胡迪尼爬过去。

四周。接着他站到墙的一侧，他的助手们会在他周围放上一块屏风，然后在另一侧也放上一块屏风。之后所有人退后，站着等待。

哈里在屏风上方挥着手，喊道：“你们看，我在这里！”然后他的手就消失了。他的助手们把屏风搬走，哈里居然不见了。片刻之后，哈里会从另一侧的屏风后走出来。

他是怎么做到的呢？台上的人没有看到他从后面绕过去，观众看到了砌墙的全过程，所以他们知道墙上也不存在暗门或通道，舞台地板上有布单，因此他也绝对无法从墙底下钻过去。

好吧，事情并不完全是这样的。事实上，他就是从墙底下钻过去的。舞台地板上有一块活板，就在墙的下面。一切就绪后，他的一个助手会躲在舞台下方，打开活板，这样墙底和布单间会形成一个通道，供哈里挤过去。哈里挤过去的时候，站在布单四周的人阻止了布单的移动，那些人以为自己是在阻止胡迪尼设计欺骗他们，实际上，他们反而是在帮助他。

哈里的另一个了不起的幻术节目并不这么容易解释。很多魔术师都能让东西“消失”，比如让一只兔子、一枚硬币甚至一个人消失。但哈里想要表演的是这世上最大的“消失”幻术，于是，他推出了他的下一个节目——消失的大象。

哈里只在大剧院里表演这个节目，因为只有大剧院有足够的空间容纳一头大象。节目一开始，哈里会先介绍他的大象，大象名叫珍妮。接着，哈里的助手们会拉来一个能装下珍妮的带轮大箱子。哈里绕着箱子走一圈，打开四面的门，让观众看到箱子后面并没有隐藏的部分。哈里把珍妮领进箱子，然后关上所有的门。

片刻后，哈里再次打开箱子的门。珍妮不见了。他再次绕箱子走一圈，将所有的门都打开。珍妮消失了！

观众惊呆了。他是如何做到的呢？诀窍在于箱子的结构。但在观众看来，哈里真的让一头大象消失了。

消失的大象

哈里领着珍妮走到台上的一个大箱子旁。

珍妮走进挂着帘子的箱口，从观众的视线中消失。

箱子由可活动的折叠板构成，将折叠板展开，观众发现里面的珍妮消失了。

诀窍

通过箱子后面的弹簧门，珍妮进入一个带轮子的笼子，珍妮接受过训练，知道走进笼子能找到自己喜欢的食物。

在箱子折叠板展开时，观众无法看到助手们正将笼子秘密移走。

第九章

成为英雄

哈里首次表演“消失的大象”是在 1918 年 1 月 1 日，地点是纽约市的一座大型建筑里，那里是个马术表演场。哈里为了给在第一次世界大战中阵亡的美国士兵的家人筹款，在此处举办了精彩的魔术表演，“消失的大象”正是其中的一个节目。哈里十分重视为士兵家人筹款这件事，因此他认为，很有必要推出一些新的，令人惊奇的节目。

1914 年，第一次世界大战在欧洲爆发，当时哈里正在美国进行巡演。在很长一段时间里，美国都没有参战。哈里取消了德国的演出，并开始和记者讲述一些故事，让自己听起来更像美国人。这是因为美国国内反德情绪高涨，哈里不想与敌方扯上任何关系。

哈里像往常一样继续巡回演出。但就哈里个人来说，这是一段悲伤的日子。1913 年 7 月 17 日，他遭受了重大打击，曾一度认为自己永远不能从打击中恢复过来。他的母亲塞西莉亚·魏斯去世了。

哈里一生都信守对父亲的承诺。他总是寄钱给母亲，照顾母亲。他母亲与哈里和贝丝一起住在纽约，直到去世。哈里也经常带着塞西莉亚去欧洲看他表演。他总是说，母亲和贝丝是他最爱的两个人。

正如哈里一直担心的那样，塞西莉亚去世时，他在欧洲。一听到消息，他就取消了剩下的巡演（包括为瑞典国王的演出），赶回家参加葬礼。在之后的人生中，他一直在哀悼她。有些遇到他的人说，这是他唯一能谈论的话题。在接下来的几年时间里，尽管他一直坚持演出，但他很悲伤，注意力也难以集中。

第一次世界大战

1914年6月28日，第一次世界大战爆发，俄罗斯、英国、意大利和法国对阵德国、奥地利和现在的土耳其。这是第一次“现代”战争，使用了机枪和坦克等可怕的新型武器。双方都很强大，武器精良，都不愿屈服。战争持续了四年多，约有一千万人丧生。

战争初期，伍德罗·威尔逊总统决定不让美国卷入战争。他告诉人们要保持中立，试图与双方保持贸易和外交关系。但在1915年5月7日，一艘德国潜艇袭击了英国的“卢西塔尼亚”号邮轮，船上有一百二十八个美国人丧生。接着在1917年初，德国潜艇开始袭击所有驶往英国的船只，包括美国船只。很快，威尔逊总统和美国别无选择，只能参战。在美国提供的军队、补给和武器的帮助下，战局扭转。最终，1918年11月，德国投降，达成和平。

幸运的是，贝丝一直陪在哈里身边，帮助哈里渡过所有难关。即使在他练习还不完善的最危险的特技表演时，她也从不怀疑他会安然无恙地回到自己身边。有时他比她还担心自己的安全。有一次，他在跳桥之前递给朋友一张纸，上面写着“我把所有一切都留给贝丝”。他想确保自己一旦发生意外，她的生活能有保障。

1917 年 4 月，美国决定参加欧洲的战争。当月，哈里报名参军。他下定决心要为实现和平尽自己的那份力量。

遗憾的是，哈里当时已经四十三岁，尽管他比许多年轻人身体素质还要好，但已经过了参军的年龄。于是，他想出了别的办法。既然数百万人愿意花钱观看自己的表演，为什么不把其中的部分收入捐出来，用来支持战争呢？

哈里为了给美国军队募捐而在全美各地演出。除此之外，他还为成千上万的士兵表演，为军营中的伤员表演。他甚至在士兵上战场前给他们上课，教他们如何逃脱德国人的手铐和锁链。哈里一直小心翼翼地保守着自己逃脱术的秘密，但此刻，他却主动透露了其中的一些诀窍。他认为如果能帮助美国赢得战争，这么做就是值得的。

“这不是‘我们会赢还是会输’的问题，”他写道，“而是我们必须赢，这才是事情的本质。”仅在纽约市的那个马术表演场（他首次表演“消失的大象”的地方），他就为美国士兵的家人筹集了近万美元。

胡迪尼一生都致力于慈善事业，包括向医院和孤儿院捐款，在那些地方免费表演。孩子们都很喜欢他，他也特别喜欢为孩子们表演。

哈里和贝丝一直没有孩子，为此哈里很难过。这也是他俩婚姻中唯一的缺憾。他忌妒他的弟弟西奥，因为西奥有儿子。但不管怎么样，贝丝和哈里在一起的生活很幸福。对他们来说，宠物就像孩子一样。他们的狗查理和他们一起旅行了八年。

胡迪尼与泰迪

虽然哈里由于工作忙碌，无法有太多的社交生活，但他和贝丝仍然有很多朋友。他喜欢结识其他名人，尤其是

查理与胡迪尼

那些知道他是谁的人。在一次往返于欧洲和美国的轮船旅行中，他的一些精彩魔术令美国前总统泰迪·罗斯福惊叹不已[①]。之后，哈里一直珍藏着他与老罗斯福总统的合影。胡迪尼也曾与查理·卓别林和巴斯特·基顿合影，这两人是默片银幕上最伟大的喜剧明星。他与《野性的呼唤》和《白牙》的作者杰克·伦敦成了好朋友。他还结识了创造了福尔摩斯这个小说人物的阿瑟·柯南·道尔爵士，但是这段友谊的结局对哈里·胡迪尼来说并不那么美好。

胡迪尼与杰克

① 泰迪·罗斯福是西奥多·罗斯福（1858—1919），美国第二十六任总统，人称老罗斯福，泰迪是他的昵称。

第十章

成为揭穿假灵媒的侦探

阿瑟·柯南·道尔爵士是英国作家，因创作以大侦探夏洛克·福尔摩斯为主角的畅销推理小说而闻名。福尔摩斯绝顶聪明，观察入微，可以通过聆听和观察一个人的言谈举止来了解这个人的方方面面。夏洛克·福尔摩斯依靠严密的逻辑推理来解开谜案，其过程有如把复杂的拼图一块块拼起来。没有人能骗过他。但是，福尔摩斯的创造者阿瑟·柯南·道尔爵士和他笔下的那个目光犀利、遇事多疑的著名主人公并不太一样。

胡迪尼和阿瑟爵士相识之时，阿瑟爵士对当时兴起的“通灵术”（也称招魂术）有着浓厚的兴趣。通灵术在第一次世界大战后的20世纪20年代非常流行，信奉通灵术的人声称他们可以与鬼魂或亡灵沟通。而一战后，许多人想要相信——也需要相信——他们能与死去的亲人联系。

阿瑟·柯南·道尔爵士

在通灵仪式上（又称为降灵会），自称灵媒的人会召集一群人围着一张桌子坐着，然后试图与死者的灵魂交流。灵媒会用许多神秘的现象来证明灵魂真的降临了，如悬浮的物体、奇怪的敲桌声、乐器自动发声等。

阿瑟爵士认为，通灵术“绝对是人类历史上最重要的发展成果”，但哈里却一个字都不信，因为他清楚与死人交谈是怎么回事。年轻的时候，他就表演过与死人交谈的节目，但他后来不再表演了，因为骗人是不对的。他坚信所有这些新冒出来的灵媒也都是假的。

阿瑟爵士对通灵术的笃信令哈里震惊。如此聪明之人，如此重视逻辑推理之人，怎么会被这样的小把戏欺

通灵术

19 世纪末，通灵术在美国变得十分流行。玛格丽特·福克斯和凯瑟琳·福克斯姐妹俩声称她们能听到有鬼魂在她们的房子里活动。姐妹俩声称，她们能理解鬼魂发出的敲击声，这些声音实际上是来自神灵界的信息。她们与鬼魂的对话演

变成了人们可以参与的表演。不久，姐妹俩开始在全国各地巡回演出，表演与其他鬼魂的“对话”。

福克斯姐妹的表演大受欢迎，吸引了成千上万的人前来观看，他们认为通灵术的兴起是一场新的宗教运动。然而，1888 年，通灵术遭到了重创，因为玛格丽特·福克斯公开承认她和妹妹是骗子，敲击声实际上是她们用脚趾发出的。她站出来揭穿这些是想让人们知道这一切都是骗局和谎言。

但是，很多人拒绝相信通灵术是假的，其中包括阿瑟爵士，他坚持认为哈里·胡迪尼真的拥有超自然能力。

骗呢？答案是：人们相信自己想要相信的东西。阿瑟爵士在第一次世界大战中失去了一个儿子。在灵媒传递了他儿子的信息之后，阿瑟爵士极度希望相信这一切是真的。柯南·道尔夫妇都非常信奉通灵术，柯南·道尔夫人还自己尝试通灵。

哈里与阿瑟爵士初次见面时，他没有说出自己的疑虑，因为他想和这个伟大的作家做朋友。除了通灵术，两人在其他方面真的相处得很好。阿瑟爵士对哈里的幻术和高超的技艺极为感兴趣，即使到了后来，那时他们已经不再和对方说话，阿瑟爵士仍告诉人们，他确信哈里有通灵的能力，不然怎么解释他的逃脱术呢？当然，哈里自己可以解释，但他不会轻易透露自己的逃脱术秘密。

两人于1920年相识，做了近两年的密友。但在1922年初，哈里出于对阿瑟爵士的欣赏，同意与他一起参加降灵会，这是个相当错误的决定。

阿瑟爵士在美国巡回演讲期间，曾和夫人住在新泽西州。胡迪尼夫妇周末拜访他们时，阿瑟爵士建议他们尝试一种叫自动书写的降灵方法。大致过程是柯南·道尔夫人会进入昏睡状态，试图与灵魂取得联系，然后她会写下灵魂“告诉”她的所有话语。阿瑟爵士认为，通过此法，他们也许能联系上哈里的母亲。

哈里听到降灵会有些不自然，但他还是同意参加。也许他内心深处真的希望能与母亲塞西莉亚沟通，毕竟他仍然非常想念她。

降灵会的结果令阿瑟爵士激动不已。他的夫人写满了十五页纸，上面全是塞西莉亚向哈里传达的信息，表达了她对他的爱和思念之情。阿瑟爵士认为哈里一定会和他一样深信不疑，因为哈里绝不可能否认这样的证据。

哈里不想惹阿瑟·柯南·道尔爵士不快。他在降灵会期间表现得彬彬有礼，对自己的怀疑只字不提。但事后，在日记和写给朋友的信中，他公开表达了他的怀疑。

他说，首先，柯南·道尔夫人写信息之前，在页面顶端画了一个十字。她说这是一个常见的“符号”，表明该灵魂是个“善灵”。但哈里认为，他的母亲是犹太人，绝不会画十字。更可疑的是，这些信息完全是用英语写的，而哈里的母亲却从未说过英语。如果她真的想给哈里传递信息，她肯定会用德语来写。

阿瑟爵士听说了哈里的评论，非常生气。胡迪尼怎么敢指责阿瑟爵士的妻子欺骗他呢？平心而论，柯南·道尔夫人可能并不想欺骗胡迪尼，她可能真的以为自己收到了塞西莉亚·魏斯的信息。原因在于她笃信通灵术，十分相信自己能与神灵界建立联系。

1922 年 4 月，哈里和阿瑟爵士开始相互写信争论起来。这场争论很快进入公众视野。新闻报纸很喜欢看到两个名人在如此热门的问题上争论。他们两人各自发表

文章，为自己的立场辩护。两人的立场总是不一致，这导致他们的友谊破裂。

在接下来的几年里，哈里花费大量的时间来揭穿假灵媒和驳斥通灵术信奉者。他甚至写了好几本通灵方面的书，其中包括《亡灵间的魔术师》，该书于 1924 年出版。他向众人挑战，请他们拿出一些他无法用魔术重现的“灵异现象”。如果有人能赢他，他愿意付一万美元。结果如他早期的“手铐挑战”一样，他从来没有付过钱。

他还在全国巡回演出，专门向大家展示那些灵媒是如何耍手段骗人的。很多降灵会都在黑暗的房间里开展，所有人围成一圈坐着，手拉着手。哈里向人们展示灵媒如何利用脚和头制造出人们在黑暗中听到的声音和看到的效果。他也展示了那些通灵人士如何轻而易举地找到人们的信息来欺骗人们。

哈里参加美国各地的降灵会。他向灵媒们提出只有他母亲才能回答出的问题。他对他们说，如果他们真能与亡灵对话，就一定能从他母亲那里得到问题的答案。有时他去前需要乔装打扮一番，因为很多灵媒一看到他在场，会拒绝举行通灵仪式。

也许哈里想要找到一个真正的灵媒。只要能再和母亲说上一次话，他愿意付出一切。他说，如果有人能说服他，他愿意承认通灵术真的存在。但哈里认为，利用谎言和欺骗手段从那些通常已经伤心欲绝、情感脆弱的人手里骗钱真的可恶万分。哈里觉得揭露这些骗局也是帮助他们的一种方式。

第十一章

永远被人铭记

很多人认为哈里死于一次高难度的逃脱术表演。事实上，1953 年曾上映一部关于他生平的电影（大部分内容是虚构的），名为《胡迪尼传》，在这部电影的情节中，他是在一次大胆鲁莽的特技表演中溺水身亡的。他的逃脱术表演固然危险，可能导致他死亡，但他并非因此而死。

1926 年 10 月 22 日上午，哈里身在加拿大蒙特利尔的麦吉尔大学。哈里的脚踝在几天前的一次逃脱术表演中骨折，因此他走起路来一瘸一拐。同时，因贝丝食物中毒，他此时身体疲惫，心情焦虑。但无论感觉到如何不舒服，他都不会放弃表演。

哈里当时在更衣室休息，别人正给他画肖像。一个大学生敲门进来，开口问了他一些有关他的问题，问题涉及生活方面、信仰方面，也有魔术方面。尽管哈里觉得很累，但他还是友好地接待了他。

这时，那个学生突然说：“胡迪尼先生，这是真的吗？您体格强壮，即使有人击打您的腹部，您也不会受伤？”

哈里的确非常强壮，但更重要的是，他知道如何控制自己身上的肌肉，这样即使有人打他，他也不会受伤，但这需要片刻的准备来收紧腹部。所以当那个学生问哈里自己能不能试着打他时，哈里说当然可以。不幸的是，哈里并没有把话当真。他还没来得及准备，那个学生的拳头就重重地打到了他的肚子上。

“嘿，住手！”房间里的其他人惊叫起来，“你疯了吗？”

哈里举起了手，那个学生停下了手上的动作。“够了。”哈里虚弱地说。

哈里疼得很厉害，但他不知道的是，那个学生不小心打破了他的阑尾。哈里的伤情非常危险，但他仍然拒绝取消演出。他是哈里·胡迪尼，他可不会因为有些肚子疼就倒下。

10 月 24 日晚，哈里在底特律进行了最后一场演出，随后便倒下了。在贝丝的坚持下，他被送进了医院。10 月 25 日，医生切除了他的阑尾。但遗憾的是，手术对哈里来说为时过晚，阑尾破裂已经导致严重感染。哈里又苦苦地支撑了几天。最后，他对弟弟西奥说：“我厌恶了战斗……不能再战斗了。”这成了他的遗言。

哈里死于万圣节那天——1926 年 10 月 31 日，享年五十二岁。数千人参加了他的盛大葬礼，之后他被安葬在纽约市皇后区的马赫佩拉墓园，就葬在他母亲旁边。

之后很多年里，贝丝一直试图联系上哈里的亡魂。哈里曾向她承诺，如果有可能回来与活着的人交谈，他会想办法联系她的。他甚至告诉了她一条暗语，让她能判断来的是否真的是他，但那条暗语从来没有出现过。

哈里死后，贝丝又活了很多年，但她从未忘记哈里，终其一生都怀念他。

哈里・胡迪尼的魔术到底是怎么回事？他是如何变出那些令人惊叹的魔术的？我们知道其中的一些秘诀。“变形魔法”和“牛奶罐逃脱术”主要依赖的是特殊的机械构造——半数的诀窍在他使用的设备上。即便如此，复制胡迪尼的魔术仍然很难，也很危险。表演中真的可能发生致命事故，但他不在乎。他热爱表演，他喜欢出名，他还喜欢成为世界上唯一一个能完成这些魔术的人。

哈里出生在一个充满新发现和新发明的时代。他热爱现代新事物，他的生活也体现了这一点，无论是驾驶飞机、拍摄电影，还是用科学手段揭穿通灵术，都体现了这种热爱。如果他活在现在，他可能会是第一个拥有自己网站的魔术师，也许正想着如何从航天飞机里逃脱呢。

年少时，哈里来到美国，像千百万其他移民一样，希望在美国实现梦想。他一生都在追寻自己的梦想，全身心地投入自己所做的每一件事情中。他向世人证明，只要努力工作并相信自己，任何人都能做到任何事。

即使到了今天，哈里·胡迪尼身上也还存在许多未解之谜。人们不禁要问，他的魔术是否存在不为人知的大秘密呢？哈里喜欢人们这么想。他的一些魔术几乎无法解释。但正如贝丝常说的：他的魔力从来都与魔术无关，完全在于他这个人，哈里·胡迪尼本人。

哈里·胡迪尼生平年表

1874 年	3 月 24 日，哈里（埃里克·魏斯）在匈牙利的布达佩斯出生。
1878 年	哈里和家人移民美国。
1886 年	哈里离家出走。
1887 年	哈里和父亲来到纽约。
1890 年	哈里读了《罗贝尔 - 乌丹回忆录》，受到启发，立志成为一名魔术师。
1892 年	10 月 5 日，哈里的父亲，犹太教拉比迈尔·沙穆埃尔·魏斯去世。
1893 年	哈里和他的弟弟西奥在芝加哥的世界博览会上表演。
1894 年	哈里与比阿特丽斯（贝丝）·雷蒙德相识、结婚。
1899 年	哈里被马丁·贝克赏识，开始在歌舞杂耍戏院表演。
1900 年	哈里与贝丝乘船前往英国，开始欧洲巡演之旅。
1902 年	哈里在英国受到威廉·霍奇森的挑战。
1905 年	哈里和贝丝返回美国。
1908 年	哈里进行首次牛奶罐逃脱术表演。
1910 年	哈里成为在澳大利亚驾驶飞机第一人。
1913 年	7 月 17 日，哈里的母亲塞西莉亚·魏斯去世。
1918 年	哈里在纽约表演“消失的大象”。
1919 年	哈里主演的首部电影《神秘的大师》上映。
1922 年	哈里参加降灵会，他与阿瑟·柯南·道尔爵士的友谊至此结束。
1924 年	哈里写的书《亡灵间的魔术师》出版。
1926 年	10 月 31 日，哈里去世。

世界大事记

1874 年 — 首次印象派画展在巴黎举办。
1879 年 — 阿尔伯特·爱因斯坦出生。
1886 年 — 自由女神像落成。
1887 年 — 阿瑟·柯南·道尔爵士出版首部福尔摩斯侦探故事。
1891 年 — 马萨诸塞州发明了篮球运动。
1892 年 — 纽约港的埃利斯岛启用。
1893 年 — 新西兰成为世界上首个允许妇女投票的国家。
1894 年 — 鲁德亚德·吉卜林出版《丛林之书》。
1899 年 — 布鲁克林儿童博物馆开馆，成为世界上第一座儿童博物馆。
1900 年 — 西格蒙得·弗洛伊德博士出版《梦的解析》。
1902 年 — 发现第一块霸王龙化石。
— 比阿特丽克斯·波特出版第一本《彼得兔的故事》。
1904 年 — 纽约地铁开放。
1908 年 — 亨利·福特开发了第一辆 T 型汽车，售价仅八百五十美元。
1910 年 — 美国童子军成立。
1913 年 — 填字游戏首次出现在《纽约世界报》上。
1922 年 — 林肯纪念堂竣工。
— 图坦卡门国王的陵墓被发现。
1923 年 — 牧羊犬任丁丁成为第一只电影明星狗。
1926 年 — 安妮·奥克利去世。

Who Was Harry Houdini?

Who was Harry Houdini?

Most people know that he was a famous magician—but did you know that he was also a movie star, a pilot, an acrobat, and a writer?

Harry Houdini (pronounced hoo-DEE-nee) didn't even really like the word "magician." He preferred to call himself an "escape artist." He said he could break out of anything—handcuffs, jail cells, straitjackets, chains, padlocked boxes, iron cages, anything! People challenged Houdini to escape from all sorts of weird things in all sorts of weird places. And he always succeeded!

Why do people still find him so fascinating? For one thing, a lot of what he did has never been done by anyone else. Many of his tricks are still mysteries. And he told so many fantastic stories about his life that sometimes it's hard to know what was true and what wasn't. We also don't know *why* he did all the crazy and dangerous things that he did. Was it to impress people? Was it because he thought it would make him rich? Or was it because he wanted to be the best in the world at *something*—and he wanted the world to know it? Harry Houdini was certainly a very talented escape artist. More importantly, he was determined. What Houdini wanted, Houdini got. And Houdini wanted attention—lots of it!

In a time before television and movies, Harry Houdini became famous all over the world. *Everybody* knew who he was. He made sure of that! Can you imagine somebody getting famous today without using TV, computers, or movies?

But being famous was very important to Houdini—and his dream came true. Even now, more than 75 years after his death, he is still the most famous magician who ever lived.

Chapter 1

So You Want to Be an American

The year was 1886. A twelve-year-old boy stood on the platform at a train station. He was small but muscular and tough-looking, with dark hair, bright blue-grey eyes, and a frown on his face.

He was not where he meant to be.

He had hopped on a train in Milwaukee, Wisconsin, several hundred miles to the north. His plan was to get to Texas—where he thought the train was going. Along the way, he had sent his mother a postcard.

But this was not Texas. The sign on the platform clearly said: "Kansas City, Missouri." Somehow, he had ended up on the wrong train. And now here he was, hundreds of miles and several states away from Texas.

What could he do?

He'd have to make the best of it. After all, he had run away from home so he could earn more money for his family. He planned to run errands, shine shoes, do any jobs he could find. Surely he could do that just as well in Missouri as he could in Texas. So off he went to town, looking for a place to sleep.

In the years to come, this boy would travel a lot farther than Kansas City, Missouri. The nickels and dimes he planned to bring home to his family would one day be hundreds and thousands of dollars. But then, at that point, the young shoeshine boy could never have imagined that one day he'd be a world-famous magician. He had trouble just earning enough money to eat!

Harry Houdini's childhood is full of stories that may or may not be true. He was born on March 24, 1874, in Budapest, Hungary. His real name was Ehrich Weiss. But during his lifetime, Harry always said his birthday was April 6, because that is what his mother told him. And sometimes he said he was born in America— depending on which reporter he was talking to!

In those days, many people in Europe thought of America as a magical place where all their problems would be solved. Thousands came to the United States from Europe hoping to make a new start in life—and lots of money, too. Harry's father was one of them.

His name was Mayer Samuel Weiss, and he was a rabbi, a teacher of the Jewish religion. It was hard to be a Jew living in Hungary, where people and laws treated them like second-class citizens and it was difficult to get a job. The Weiss family was very poor. Samuel thought that perhaps he could do better in America. After all, people called it the "land of opportunity." So in 1876, when Ehrich was two years old, Samuel left his wife and sons in Hungary. Although he did not speak a word of English, he set off for America, on the other side of the ocean. It took him two years to save enough money to bring over his family.

Can you imagine what that trip must have been like? First, Harry's mother, Cecilia, and her four sons would have had to get from Hungary to a port city. From there they would board a ship, along with as many as two thousand other people bound for America. Big ships like these took anywhere from two weeks to two months to cross the Atlantic Ocean. The passengers had to deal with crowded conditions and limited food. For the rest of his life, Houdini hated traveling by boat.

The Statue of Liberty now stands in New York City's harbor welcoming newcomers to the United States. But it wasn't built yet when Ehrich and the Weiss family arrived. America was a big, strange, new world—and now it was Ehrich's new home.

Unfortunately, life wasn't much easier in the United States. From New York, the Weisses went to live in Wisconsin, first in a small town called Appleton, and later in the city of Milwaukee. When he was only eight years old, Ehrich started working to help pay the bills. He sold newspapers, shined shoes, and ran errands. At age nine, he also had his first starring act in a backyard circus that he put together with his friends. He called himself "The Prince of the Air" and did stunts on a homemade trapeze hung from a tree. Later, he made up stories for reporters about this time. He would either say he had been in a real traveling circus as a boy, or that he was already performing his famous escapes at age nine! The truth is he wasn't really interested in magic yet. But he liked the acrobatics—and the applause.

Not much is known about Ehrich's adventures as a runaway, except that he definitely left home for a while when he was twelve. He may have run away from home more than once, even though he loved his family very much. He always planned to return once he had some money.

Living and traveling on his own made Ehrich resourceful

and clever. So when Samuel moved to New York City in 1887, hoping for better luck there, he picked thirteen-year-old Ehrich to take with him (even though he wasn't the oldest son). Together they raised enough money so that the rest of the family could join them.

But Samuel Weiss died in 1892, leaving his wife with six children to care for. Still, Ehrich was sure he could help out his family. America had not been the land of opportunity for his father, but Ehrich was determined that it would be for him.

Also, before he died, his dad made Ehrich promise something—to always take care of his mother. Ehrich took any promise very seriously, and this one most of all. For the rest of her life, Cecilia Weiss could depend on her "truant son."

There' s one story about his childhood that Harry Houdini loved to tell in later years. Whether or not it's true, it certainly sounds like his style. One day in December, while

Ehrich was working as a messenger boy, he had an idea. He wrote out a card and stuck it to his hat.

The words on the card were:

Christmas is coming

Turkeys are fat

Please drop a quarter

In the Messenger Boy's hat.

Lots of people laughed and gave him quarters. That night, when he got home, he hid all the quarters in his hair and in his clothes. Then he went to his mother and said, "Shake me! I'm magic!" So she did. Quarters came flying out and went rolling all over the place—like magic!

Then, when he was about sixteen, Ehrich came across a book called *The Memoirs of Robert-Houdin, Ambassador, Author, and Conjuror, Written by Himself.* It was the autobiography of a very famous nineteenth-century French magician. It was full of fantastic stories. Ehrich was hooked.

If Robert- Houdin could become so famous through magic, then Ehrich Weiss could, too! But he'd need a catchy stage name. His family called him "Ehrie" (short for Ehrich). That sounded like Harry. And "Houdin" was a name that already made people think of magic. So Harry added an "i" to the end, and tada! Harry Houdini was born.

Robert - Houdin

Before Jean-Eugène Robert-Houdin (1805–1871), magic shows were performed in outdoor markets or on street corners. Robert- Houdin made magic into an art by doing tricks no one had thought of before. He used new scientific developments in his tricks. (He had started off as a clockmaker!) Like Harry Houdini, Robert-Houdin was very modern. He studied electromagnetism, so he could use powerful magnets to move objects around the stage.

Robert- Houdin was also really clever at promoting himself. His autobiography (published in 1857) was full of exaggerations and wild stories. His skill and style, however, were so successful that, even today, Robert-Houdin is still considered to be "the father of modern magic."

Chapter 2

So You Want to Be a Magician

Success didn't come "like magic" for Harry. How does someone become a magician, after all? It's not like becoming a doctor or a lawyer. There is no school for magicians. It took Harry years of hard work.

First, of course, a magician has to learn lots of tricks. Harry was always looking for new tricks and illusions, even after he became very famous. He watched other magicians, read books on magic, and wrote everything down in notebooks. He always kept a notebook by his bed in case he thought of something in the middle of the night.

Being a magician also takes practice, practice, and more practice. Harry practiced his tricks over and over again. He did special exercises to keep his hands and feet flexible and fast. He carried a coin with him and flipped it through his fingers whenever he wasn't performing. Try it—it's harder than it looks!

But beyond just learning and practicing, Harry also had to work on selling himself. Even the best magician needs an audience. Harry had to find ways to make people come and see his act. He had to get people's attention.

One of Harry's first magic acts was called "The Brothers Houdini." His younger brother, Theo, was his partner. They did card tricks and mind reading, disappearing acts and illusions.

An illusion is something that seems to have happened but logically couldn't have. For instance, have you ever seen a magician pull a coin out of someone's ear? That's an illusion. Or a magician rips a sheet of paper into bits, then—presto!—it is all back in one piece. Logically, it's not possible for the paper to put itself back together, or for a magician to find a coin in someone's ear. But the trick is done so quickly that it looks real to the people watching.

Harry and Theo did a lot of these kinds of tricks. They did their act anywhere they could find a place to put on their show. And they always set aside money to send home to their mother. One of the most exciting places they performed was in the sideshow at the 1893 World's Fair in Chicago. Harry was just nineteen and Theo was seventeen.

Theo and Harry got along well. Theo was a lot like Harry in some ways—he loved magic too. (He later had a career on his own as a magician.) But there were problems. One night, Theo messed up their best trick. Harry hated mistakes. He insisted on everything being perfect in front of an audience. Theo just couldn't keep up with him. Harry needed a replacement for Theo—and soon enough, one came along.

In the summer of 1894, the Brothers Houdini performed in the same town as a song-and-dance act called the Floral

Sisters. One of the sisters was a tiny, brown-haired girl called Beatrice Raymond. Like Harry, she had changed her name to go on stage. Her real name was Wilhelmina Rahner. But everyone called her Bess. She was eighteen years old. Harry was twenty.

For Bess and Harry, it was love at first sight. Some stories say they got married only two weeks after they met. According to one of these stories, Bess had to sneak out of her house to go on a date with Harry because she was worried her mother would be mad. Later that evening, she told him she was scared to go home. So he proposed right then and there, and they got married that night! Even if that's not true, they certainly fell in love and got married quickly. It's also true that Bess's mother wasn't happy about it. Bess's family was Catholic. Harry was Jewish, the son of a rabbi. But Harry's mother didn't mind. She thought Bess was just wonderful. And so did Harry.

Bess was more than a perfect wife; she was an ideal

stage partner, too. Already used to performing, she was happy to sing and dance between Harry's acts, and she would always announce him with great style. She also learned the tricks quickly, so she could help him with everything.

Bess was tiny—only five feet tall! That made even Harry look big, and he was only about 5′5″ or 5′6″. Her size also meant she could slip in and out of tight places, which was very useful for escape tricks.

Even later on, when Harry did solo shows, Bess traveled with him everywhere. She managed his schedule, kept track of his performances, and made sure he remembered to change his shirt every day. Harry said she was the reason for his fame: "She brought me luck and it has been with me ever since. I never had any before I married her." Harry and Bess were together until the day he died.

In the 1890s, Harry, with help from Bess, performed in large halls called dime museums. For ten cents people could enter and watch strange and bizarre acts—sword-swallowers, performing monkeys, jugglers. Houdini would do his Metamorphosis trick.

A small, serious-looking young man in a shabby tuxedo, Houdini stood on a box, waving to the crowds. With him was Bess, wearing woolen tights and a puffy white blouse.

First Harry would pick a few people out from the audience—a “committee” to examine the “apparatus”. The apparatus was a tall cabinet with a trunk inside. The trunk was big enough to hold a person. The committee had to inspect the trunk. They knocked on all its sides. They looked inside. Finally they would announce that everything seemed to be normal—no hidden doors or anything.

Then Harry gave the committee a large black bag and some heavy tape. Following his instructions, they tied his hands together, helped him into the bag, and taped the bag shut as tightly as they could. Then the bag with Harry inside was put in the trunk. The trunk was also locked, tied securely with heavy ropes, and placed inside the cabinet.

Metamorphosis Trick

The apparatus is inspected by the committee.

Harry is placed in a sack and trunk as attendants tie his hands and close the sack.

The trunk is tied with strong rope and locked with a heavy chain. The trunk is placed in the cabinet.

Bess closes the curtain in front of the cabinet, addresses the audience, claps three times, and steps behind the curtain.

When the curtain is opened, Harry is standing next to the trunk.

He then opens the trunk and sack to reveal Bess.

How It's Done

Harry unties his hands, cuts through the

bottom of the sack with a hidden knife, and crawls out a sliding panel on the back of the trunk. Bess then crawls through the panel and into the sack, replacing Harry.

Once this was all done, Bess closed the curtain in front of the cabinet.

"Now, ladies and gentlemen," she would say, pausing dramatically, "I shall clap my hands three times, and on my last clap I ask you to watch ... closely ..." As she clapped, she stepped behind the curtain. Not three seconds later, the curtain swept open. And who was standing there before the audience? Harry Houdini! But what happened to Bess?

Harry turned to the trunk, which was still sealed shut. With the help of the committee, he untied and unlocked the trunk to reveal the bag. And when they opened the bag—there was Bess, tied up the same way Harry had been!

This was the same trick that Theo had messed up once before. But Bess was smaller. And she was so quick that she could do it in no time at all, exactly the way Harry wanted. The change—or "metamorphosis"—happened so fast, it looked like real magic!

Chapter 3

So You Want to Be Famous

Metamorphosis was an amazing illusion, but it wasn't enough to make "The Houdinis" as famous as Harry wanted to be. The show needed to add something new and dramatic.

Harry tried a lot of different things. With Bess, he did mind-reading acts, circus acrobatics, and even faked "talking to the dead" a few times. How did he talk to the dead? Research and cleverness. When they got to a new town, Harry read local newspapers. He'd go to the graveyard to see who had just died. He listened to people tell stories about friends. Then, on stage, he would use this information to make people think he was really talking to ghosts. It was very believable to the audience. Houdini gave up "talking to the dead" after only a few performances, however. He didn't like the idea of tricking people this way. It was not the same as "magic" where the audience knew that some illusion or trick had to be involved.

Luckily, Harry finally did find something unique to make him famous: escapes. Other magicians had used handcuffs in their acts before Houdini, but he was the first who made it the main attraction of his show. He was also the first person to try escaping from a straitjacket in front of an audience.

Straitjackets are complicated coats with straps and buckles. They are used to keep someone violent from hurting himself or others. A person in a straitjacket can't use their arms and hands at all. Harry thought that he could get out of one. After a lot of practice and effort, he really could. And it looked impressive on stage! He decided not to hide behind a curtain for this part of the show, because it wasn't a trick at all. It just took a lot of skill and effort (and practice). Even after watching him do it, the audience couldn't really explain how it was done—and certainly no one else could do it!

Harry also came up with a really terrific way to promote his act. Whenever he and Bess arrived in a new town, he'd go straight to the local police station.

"I am Harry Houdini, King of Handcuffs!" he would announce. "Lock me up, tie me up, put any and all of your handcuffs on me. I guarantee you I will escape in no time at all."

The police officers usually laughed at him. Who did this short guy with the big mouth think he was? They'd never heard of any "Harry Houdini." Everybody figured that magicians used trick handcuffs. Nobody could escape from real handcuffs. They were so sure of this that they let Harry bring reporters from the local paper to watch. The police officers would search Harry for tools. (Sometimes they even insisted he do his trick naked—so they could be sure he wasn't hiding any keys in his clothing.) Then they would tie

Escaping From a Straltjacket

Expand chest and shoulders as jacket is being tightened.

Deflate chest and shoulders and work arms up and over the head.

With the arms loose you can now work open the buckles on back of jacket until free.

him up, snap a few pairs of handcuffs on his hands and feet, and leave him alone in a room, or lock him in one of their jail cells.

"We'll come back and let you out in a little while," the policemen joked. Then they'd sit in the next room to talk about this crazy show-off. Imagine their surprise a couple of minutes later. In walked Harry, holding the handcuffs up in one hand. Sometimes he was able to free himself in less than a minute.

The policemen and the news reporters were amazed. They couldn't figure out how he had done it. Harry didn't get paid for these stunts, but that didn't matter because of all the stories in the newspapers. The attention made people come to his show. They wanted to see the magician who could trick their own policemen.

The trouble was that this only worked in one town at a time. He could do this in a small city in Missouri, and be a big hit for one night. But as soon as he moved on to the next place, he'd be Mr. Nobody again, and he'd have to start all over. Remember, there was no television or Internet. It was hard to spread news around the country, especially about one small magic act.

By 1899, Harry and Bess had been on the road together for five long years. Harry was becoming discouraged. He started offering to sell his magic secrets. He even thought of quitting the magic business altogether. Then, just in the nick of time, Harry was discovered.

A man saw the Houdinis performing one night. He said to Harry, "Hey, that's quite a show you've got there. Tell you what—leave out the card tricks and paper-tearing illusions. Just give me twenty minutes of escapes, including 'Metamorphosis,' and I'll make you famous."

So who was this man? He was Martin Beck, in charge of the famous Orpheum Circuit. The Orpheum Circuit was a nationwide chain of theaters—or "vaudeville houses."

Vaudeville houses were a lot classier than dime

museums. Each night there was a show with many different acts: singers, dancers, acrobats, comedians, and so on. Martin saw that Harry's act would be perfect for vaudeville. It was new, it was different, and it was exciting. He thought Harry could be a huge success. Of course, Harry had always thought so, too.

They were right. Almost overnight, Harry became a sensation. He finally had time to focus on what he was best at—escapes. By the end of 1899, he was earning over $100 a week, which was a lot of money back then. Best of all, he was getting the attention he had always dreamed of.

Now, not only was Harry ready for the world, but the world was ready for him.

Chapter 4

So You Want to Be a Star

After fourteen months, the stages of the Orpheum Circuit theaters began to seem small to Harry. It was no longer enough for him to be a success in America. To be a real star, Harry Houdini had to conquer Europe.

In May of 1900, twenty-two years after coming to America, he crossed the Atlantic again, this time in the other direction, with Bess and their dog, Charlie. It was still a long trip (the faster ships took two weeks). He was terribly seasick the whole time. But that didn't stop Harry from performing card tricks for the other passengers.

Harry began his European tour in England. Of course, when Harry and Bess first arrived, nobody had ever heard of

Harry Houdini. He had to start selling himself all over again. But this time, it didn't take long. The "King of Handcuffs" baffled London's top police force, Scotland Yard, by escaping from their handcuffs. The news of this feat got Houdini into London's top theater, the Alhambra.

The Alhambra was the most impressive stage Harry had ever performed on. It looked more like an opera house than a vaudeville hall. The audiences were more elegant and reserved. In America, Harry had received some bad reviews because of mistakes in grammar and shabby costumes. Now he appeared every night in a formal tuxedo with a white bow tie. He polished his speech so he sounded more dignified, but still dramatic. And he kept practicing and thinking of new tricks to add to his act.

All of it worked. Audiences loved Houdini. Harry performed at the Alhambra for all of July and August, and then came back at Christmas, too. Originally, the plan had been for Harry to do a few shows in Europe and then return to America. As it turned out, Harry and Bess ended up staying in Europe for five years.

The Houdinis toured many countries in Europe. Everywhere they went, Harry tried to learn some of the language, so he could speak it during his show. This was easiest in Germany, because he had grown up speaking German with his parents. German audiences adored him, and he was a huge success there. It was dangerous, though. The German police sometimes locked up entertainers for "deceiving the public." Performers had to have their act approved by the police.

Houdini had to "audition" in front of three hundred policemen. They provided all the locks and searched Harry for keys beforehand. To protect the secrecy of his act, they let him perform it under a blanket. Of course, he escaped easily—in just six minutes! Since the police couldn't explain how he did it, they let him go on with his show.

Harry's hardest test came in a town called Blackburn, in

England. At the time, Harry was offering twenty-five British pounds—a lot of money—to anyone whose cuffs he couldn't escape from. On October 24, 1902, in the middle of his act, a man suddenly walked up on stage. His name was William Hodgson, and he wanted to take Harry up on his bet. Right away Harry was suspicious of Hodgson's handcuffs. They looked like they had been damaged, maybe even broken—making them harder to unlock. But Hodgson teased him, saying Houdini was afraid to take a real challenge. Harry Houdini would never stand for that.

Hodgson was a physical fitness expert who had carefully studied the human body and how all the muscles work. He knew exactly how to tie a man up so that he would not be able to move at all. And this is what he did to Houdini, using chains and six pairs of handcuffs. People watching were worried that Harry's circulation would be cut off completely, or that Hodgson might break Harry's bones twisting his arms around so roughly. But the hardest part for Harry was that his escape skills depended on his strength and flexibility. If he couldn't move a muscle, those skills couldn't help him.

The audience waited for a terrifying hour and a half while Houdini struggled behind the curtain. At one point, Harry asked for his wrists to be unlocked just for a minute, because his hands had gone numb and he couldn't feel them anymore. Hodgson refused, saying "If you are beaten, just give in." Harry Houdini, beaten? Impossible! Back behind the curtain he went.

Just after midnight, suddenly the curtain was thrown back. There was Harry, triumphantly flinging the last of the handcuffs down on the stage. One reporter later said he looked "as though some tiger had clawed him." He was bleeding and bruised all over, but he was free. The crowd went totally crazy.

Another incident in England drew headlines. A newspaper called the *London Daily Illustrated Mirror* challenged Houdini to escape from a single pair of "the most difficult handcuffs ever invented." How could Harry say no?

The Mirror Cuffs, as they were called, were made by a man in Birmingham, England, who claimed it had taken five years to make them. As Houdini knew from years of studying locksmiths, most locks involve simple mechanisms. They can be undone using a few basic keys or even a sharp tap in the right place. But these handcuffs were several thousand times more complicated. Only one key in the world could unlock them—and that key belonged to the man who made them.

For days before the show, newspapers ran stories about the Mirror Cuffs and the challenge. Harry loved it; the more attention he got, the better. Finally, the big night came. Harry appeared onstage to a standing ovation. As usual, a committee from the audience was chosen to make sure everything was fair. The *Mirror* reporter snapped the cuffs onto Harry's wrists, and the locksmith turned the key six times.

Harry announced, "I am now locked up in handcuffs

that have taken a British mechanic five years to make. I do not know whether I am going to get out of it or not, but I can assure you I am going to do my best."

Harry disappeared behind a curtain on stage. For a long time, the audience saw nothing but the curtain moving every now and then.

This was another interesting thing about Harry's act. Most of it took place behind a curtain, with the audience waiting for something to happen. Can you imagine going to a show today and spending most of the time staring at a curtain? Audiences were a lot more patient back then. And Harry was so magnetic and dazzling on stage that even the few minutes he did appear made the whole rest of the show worth it. Besides, there was always the question: Would he be able to escape? Or—would he fail?

After several minutes with the Mirror Cuffs, Harry came out from behind the curtain, looking exhausted. Had he escaped? No! He wanted a cushion, to rest his knees on. Then he went back.

Soon he stepped out again. But wait—he was still handcuffed! This time he asked for the handcuffs to be unlocked for a minute, so that he could take off his coat. The *Mirror* representative said no. Watching the handcuffs being unlocked might give Harry clues about how to escape from them. The cuffs would stay on until Harry admitted defeat.

Admit defeat? Harry Houdini? Never! Right onstage, using his teeth and twisting his arms around, Harry managed to get a small penknife from his jacket pocket. Dramatically, he flipped his coat over his head and, with the knife in his teeth, slashed at his coat until it fell to the floor in pieces. He tossed his head proudly, turned, and disappeared behind the curtain again.

Only ten minutes later—Harry leapt out, holding the Mirror Cuffs high over his head. He had done it. The King of Handcuffs had triumphed! The crowd went wild, and the story stayed in the newspapers for days. It had taken five years to make the handcuffs. But it had taken Houdini only one hour to escape from them.

Harry had many more adventures in Europe. In Paris, he went and visited the grave of his hero, Jean Eugène Robert-Houdin. In fact, he visited the graves of lots of famous magicians and always left big wreaths of flowers for them. He also visited many well-known, retired magicians. Some of them even shared their secrets with him, impressed by his success and charm.

Perhaps the least welcoming country Harry traveled to was Russia. As a Jew, he wasn't allowed in on his own passport. The Houdinis had to use Bess's passport and papers, because she was a Roman Catholic.

It also made him realize more than anywhere else how many people hated Jews. This kind of prejudice, anti-Semitism, was part of the reason his family had left Europe so many years before.

For the most part, however, Harry loved Europe. Even

after months in one city, he could still sell out shows every night. In America, he would have been traveling to a new place every week or so. He was also making an astonishing amount of money in Europe. Still, Harry really missed his mother. He sent money to her all the time and visited her twice between 1900 and 1905. But he wanted to be closer to her. And he didn't want America to forget about him. So, in 1905, America saw the return of Harry Houdini—huge international star.

Chapter 5

So You Want to Be Amazing

From then on, there was no stopping Harry Houdini. He went all over America, and all over the world. He challenged anyone to lock him into something he couldn't get out of. And he escaped from some pretty strange things—including a giant football! He also added a new element to his show: water.

In 1908, Houdini debuted an entirely new trick—one that he said was "the best I have ever invented!" The audience in the theater was on the edge of their seats. Harry had started off the show with some of his standard acts—illusions, Metamorphosis, handcuff escapes. Now he turned and walked downstage toward the audience. Stepping over the footlights at the bottom of the stage, he leaned forward as if he was about to leap into the first row of seats, and spread his arms wide.

"LADIES AND GENTLEMEN!" Harry boomed. His voice carried to the back row. This wasn't the shabbily dressed, quiet boy of the dime museum days. His personality electrified the theater. "Now, for the first time ever, here today I introduce to you my latest and greatest escape, the most amazing act ever seen on an American stage!"

With a flourish, Harry revealed a giant iron milk can, large enough for a small person to squeeze into. He thumped it on all sides to show how sturdy it was. Then he went offstage to change into a bathing suit, while his assistants filled the can to the brim with water.

Finally, Harry climbed into the can. "As I am submerged in water," he said to the audience, "try timing yourselves, too, to see how long you can hold your breath." He also pointed to one of his assistants, holding a large axe. "In case something goes terribly wrong, do not fear. My loyal assistant will smash open the can and free me ... let's just hope it's in time!"

With a grin, Houdini allowed himself to be handcuffed and squeezed into the can. His assistants locked down the steel cover with massive padlocks. In later versions of this escape, Harry would also invite audience members to bring their own padlocks, to close the cover even more securely.

A curtain was drawn in front of the can. People in the audience held their breath. The seconds passed ... a whole minute went by. By this point, most of the people watching were gasping for air. It is very dangerous to hold your breath for that long. And still there was no sign of Houdini. Another minute passed, then another. The audience was frantic. What if Houdini had drowned? How would anyone know? "Let him out!" they started calling. "Smash open the can, he's drowning!"

Then suddenly, Harry swept aside the curtain and

bowed. He was dripping wet and gasping for breath, but alive and free. And the can stood there, still padlocked securely.

It was a sensational trick. The audience couldn't get enough of it. And Harry liked playing with people's minds, too, to make the escape seem more dramatic. Sometimes he would get out of the can in a couple of minutes, and then wait behind the curtain for up to half an hour, letting the tension build. Once everyone was terrified that the trick hadn't worked, and that Houdini was dead, then he'd make his dramatic entrance to thunderous applause.

Harry had always been a good swimmer and comfortable in the water. He also practiced a lot for this very dangerous trick. He'd fill a bathtub with water and have Bess time him to see how long he could stay under. Or he'd make the water freezing cold and see how long he could stand it. This was useful for another new and even more dangerous trick—his river escapes.

For this act, Harry would usually start on a bridge,

surrounded by thousands of spectators (and reporters, of course!). He would strip down to a bathing suit or long underwear and allow policemen to lock him into two or more pairs of handcuffs. Then he'd climb up on the railing, wave, shout farewell to the crowd, and leap off the bridge into the freezing water. Splash! The audience hung over the railing, searching the water. Sometimes Houdini would pop right back up, holding the handcuffs triumphantly over his head. Or sometimes he would stay underwater longer, making everybody wait. A couple of times, he even swam off underwater to someplace where he could hide.

Harry always said that these were his most dangerous escapes. He warned other people not to try them. But people did anyway, and some of them died. Not only was the water dangerously cold, but sometimes the current would pull Houdini away from the boat where his assistants were waiting to help him out. Once he got trapped under ice, after the current swept him away from the hole he'd jumped through.

Houdini kept coming up with new and more dangerous twists for his underwater escapes. Sometimes he'd attach large, heavy objects to his handcuffs, so he'd get pulled down to the bottom of the water faster. Or sometimes after being tied up, he'd also be nailed inside a wooden box, which was then dropped in the river.

He did bridge jumps in cities all over the U.S., from Rochester, New York, to Boston, Massachusetts, to New Orleans, Louisiana. There was no way to charge money for these kinds of stunts, but Harry didn't mind. As with his earlier police challenges, he was excited by the fame and attention. It wasn't hard to advertise himself now. Tens of thousands of people would come out to see one of his jumps.

There was nothing Houdini liked better than a big crowd!

Chapter 6

So You Want to Be a Pilot

Harry loved being famous. He liked being the best. He also liked being *first*.

Airplanes came into use during Harry's lifetime. He was already almost thirty years old when the Wright Brothers made history in 1903 by flying the first plane at Kitty Hawk, North Carolina. Planes were dangerous, unpredictable machines, with few of the safety features they have now. Harry hated boats, and he couldn't even drive. But the very first time Harry saw a plane, he knew he had to learn to fly. Not only that: he had to be a part of aviation history.

The Wright Brothers' first flight lasted only about twelve seconds. By 1909, not even six years later, someone had already flown across the English Channel between England and France. Someone had been the first to fly at night, the first to fly with passengers, the first to fly in France, in Germany, in Italy. It was getting hard to find something new and historical to do, even for an experienced pilot. And Harry was a beginner. Yet he still was determined to make his mark as an airplane pilot. So he came up with a plan.

In January of 1910, Harry and Bess found themselves on board a massive steamship. They would be on this boat for over a month, despite Harry's seasickness. What convinced him to take an ocean voyage this long? Where were they going?

Australia.

Thousands of miles from anywhere Harry had been before, Australia was still a new, developing land. Hardly any performer of his fame was willing to make the long trip to the Southern continent. But Australia was also one place where nobody had flown a plane yet. Harry could be the first.

THE WRIGHT BROTHERS

Almost five hundred years ago, Leonardo da Vinci tried to design machines that would let people fly. But nobody built a successful one until December 17, 1903, when two brothers from Ohio finally took to the skies in a small plane they built themselves.

Orville and Wilbur Wright owned a bicycle shop, and working on bicycles taught them how important balance is—both for riding a bike and flying a plane. They realized that it would take a lot of research to design an airplane, so they decided to do their own studies and calculations. Although neither had graduated from high school, they taught themselves everything they needed to know about flight, wind, physics—anything that would be useful. They even built their own engine so that it would be exactly the right size and weight for their plane.

And finally, on that cold December day in Kitty Hawk, North Carolina, their plane took off. The first flight lasted only twelve seconds, but it was a historical turning point that forever changed the world.

Harry bought himself a plane called a Voisin. He hired a mechanic and packed everything onto the steamship with him. All through the monthlong journey, no matter how sick he felt, Harry could think about his plane stowed safely below.

Once in Australia, Harry had to fit in flying time around his demanding performance schedule. And there were always problems. Planes were still fragile machines, so he couldn't try flying when it was very windy, or foggy, or if it rained too much. Harry had to wait more than a month before he and his plane actually got off the ground.

On the morning of March 18, 1910, a group of reporters watched nervously as Harry drove the plane slowly around the field. After a few short hops into the air to make sure everything was in order, Harry pointed the plane at the far end of the field. His whole body was tense and shaking. But he was determined. He accelerated forward ... going faster ... and faster ... until up into the air he went!

Official records say that this, the first real flight in Australia, lasted about three and a half minutes, and the plane rose as high as one hundred feet in the air. That was enough to make the record books, and enough for Harry. Although he flew a few more times in Australia, his interest died. Once he and Bess left Australia, he never flew again. "I had had my adventure in the air," was how Harry explained it.

A few years later, Harry Houdini got to meet the famous Orville Wright. It turned out that Orville knew more about Harry's flying experience than about Houdini's magic!

Chapter 7

So You Want to Be a Movie Star

Soon enough, Harry found something else new to capture his interest. The early 1900s introduced the first movies to be seen in theaters. Harry was twenty-one when the first movie was shown on a big screen in a theater in Paris. These early movies were black and white, and silent, with music provided by live orchestras. The movies were very short and the action looked very jumpy. Still, people all over the world were fascinated by them. Of course, Harry never missed an opportunity to make himself more famous. What could be more perfect than a movie career?

Harry's first movie was called *The Master Mystery*. It opened in theaters in 1919. It was a serial. That meant it was shown in weekly installments, instead of all at once—more like a television show than a movie. In serials, each week's episode ended with a thrilling cliffhanger; for example, with the heroine tied to the tracks in front of an oncoming train. The audience would have to come back a week later to find out whether the star escaped or not—and how.

It's almost as if this kind of moviemaking was designed with Harry Houdini in mind. His whole career was about getting into situations that seemed impossible to escape from. Each episode of *The Master Mystery* ended with Harry trapped and in terrible danger. Then the next one began with his escape, so he could go after "the bad guys." Sounds like a great TV show, doesn't it? Now audiences could see some of Houdini's famous escapes on screen.

Careful not to give away his secrets, the movie did show how much skill and strength were involved in the escapes. For instance, in one scene Harry's hands were chained to a wall. So he used his toes like fingers—reaching for a ring of

Movies

In the late 1800s, people all over the world were racing to be the first to invent the movie camera. Thomas Edison invented one; in France, Louis Lumière invented a better camera that was lightweight and portable.

The first movie, filmed by Louis and his brother Auguste, showed factory workers at the end of a workday. The funny thing is that the Lumière brothers didn't think there was any future in moviemaking! They couldn't imagine why people would watch moving images of things they could see in the real world every day. They had no idea how popular movies were going to become.

Silent movies were very popular across the United States by 1910. The first serial movies were released in 1913. Sound in movies was not introduced until 1927, one year after Houdini's death. And the first full-length feature film in color was *Becky Sharp,* which came out in 1935.

keys, picking out the right key, and unlocking the door to his cell.

The plot of the movie was very complicated, but exciting. Harry played an undercover agent for the government, and the villain was a robot. Even though it was obvious that there was a human inside the robot outfit, it was still a new and interesting twist for a movie. *The Master Mystery* featured the first robot villain in movie history.

The Master Mystery was an international hit. People in places like India and Japan saw Harry Houdini for the first time. Of course, most of the people who saw the movie already knew who he was. By this point, Houdini didn't really need a movie to increase his fame. But he loved the attention, and people loved watching him. Harry was ready to make more movies.

Houdini starred in four more films over the next four years. But each one made less and less money. After *The Master Mystery*, Houdini switched to starring in full-length feature films, not serials. Perhaps that was part of the problem—audiences weren't left in the same state of suspense week after week. *The Grim Game, Terror Island, The Man From Beyond,* and *Haldane of the Secret Service* all got terrible reviews. Most critics agreed: Harry was a terrific escape artist who couldn't act at all.

The biggest problem, though, was that there was no way for the audience to tell the real Houdini escapes from escapes created by camera tricks. Although Harry did most of his own stunts, moviegoers knew how easy it was to fake "danger" on screen. The nature of Harry's act made it much more thrilling when it was seen live.

Still, Harry got to be a movie star, and he even got a star on the Hollywood Walk of Fame.

Chapter 8

So You Want to Be an Illusionist

As Harry got older, some of his escapes became harder for him to perform. First he cut out handcuff tricks from his act; other performers were copying those tricks anyway. Then he started replacing his dangerous escapes with big, remarkable illusions.

Most magicians, including Harry, start their careers with illusions. A classic example is pulling a rabbit out of a hat. Harry wanted to take illusions to a whole new level. And he did.

One of his new illusions used screens and an actual brick wall. Harry would have a team of bricklayers build a wall down the center of the stage, right in front of the audience. The stage floor was covered with a large sheet, pinned underneath the wall, and Harry would ask volunteers to come up and stand around the edges of the sheet. Then he would stand on one side of the wall, and his assistants would put a screen around him. They would put another screen on the other side of the wall. Then everyone would stand back and wait.

Harry, waving his hand over the top of the screen, would call, "You see, I am over here!" Then the hand would disappear, his assistants would take away the screen, and—no Harry. A moment later, Harry would walk out from behind the screen—on the other side of the wall.

How did he do it? The people onstage could see that he hadn't walked around the back. The audience had seen the wall being built, so they knew there wasn't a secret door or way through it. And surely the sheet on the stage floor guaranteed that he hadn't somehow gone under the wall.

Well, not exactly. In actual fact, that's just what he did.

Brick Wall Trick

A sheet is laid on the stage floor and a brick wall is built on a wheeled frame.

Audience volunteers inspect the wall as assistants place screens on both sides of the wall.

Houdini moves behind the screen on one side of the wall and then emerges from the other side.

The Trick

An assistant releases a trap door below the stage, allowing the sheet to sag just enough for Houdini to crawl beneath the wall.

There was a trapdoor in the stage just under the wall. Once everything was in place, one of his assistants would hide under the stage and open the trapdoor. There was just enough room for Harry to squeeze between the bottom of the wall and the sheet. Everyone standing on the sheet kept it from moving while Harry squeezed through. They thought they were preventing Houdini from tricking them. Instead, they were actually helping him.

Another of Harry's great illusions cannot be explained so easily. A lot of magicians make things "disappear"—a rabbit, a coin, even a person. But Harry wanted to perform the biggest disappearing act in the whole world. That's how he came up with his next trick: The Vanishing Elephant.

Harry performed this illusion only in the biggest theaters where there was room on stage for an elephant. He would start out by introducing his elephant who was named Jenny. Then Harry's assistants would roll in a very large box on wheels, large enough to hold Jenny. Harry would

Vanishing Elephant

Harry leads Jenny the elephant to a large box on the stage.

Jenny enters the box through the curtains and is out of the audience's view.

The box is folded open to reveal that Jenny has vanished.

The Trick

Through spring doors at the rear of the box, Jenny enters a hidden cage on wheels, where Jenny is trained to find her favorite foods.

With the box open, the audience does not see the assistants removing the secret cage.

walk around the box, opening the doors on all sides, so the audience could see that there were no hidden sections at the back. Harry would lead Jenny inside and close all the doors.

A few seconds later, Harry would sweep open the doors again. Jenny was gone. Once again, he'd walk around the box and open all the doors. She had vanished!

Audiences were amazed. How did he do it? The trick was in the construction of the box. But as far as the audience could tell, Harry had made an elephant disappear.

Chapter 9

So You Want to Be a Hero

The first time Harry performed the Vanishing Elephant trick was on January 1, 1918, in a giant building called the Hippodrome, in New York City. It was part of a spectacular magic show that Harry put on to raise money for the families of American soldiers killed in World War I. This was something that Harry cared about a lot, so it was important to him to do something new and amazing.

World War I broke out in Europe in 1914, while Harry was on tour in America. For a long time, the United States stayed out of the war. Harry cancelled his shows in Germany. He also started telling reporters stories that made him sound more American. That was because of all the anti-German feeling in the country. Harry did not want to be associated with the enemy.

Harry kept touring and performing as usual. But it was a sad time, personally, for Harry. On July 17, 1913, he suffered "a shock from which I do not think recovery is possible." His mother, Cecilia Weiss, died.

All his life, Harry had kept his promise to his father. He always sent money home to his mother and took care of her. She lived with Harry and Bess in New York City till her dying day. Often Harry had brought Cecilia along to Europe to see him perform. He always said that his mother and Bess were his two sweethearts.

Just as Harry had always feared, Cecilia died while he was away in Europe. As soon as he heard the news, he cancelled the rest of the tour (including a performance for the king of Sweden) and rushed home for the funeral. For the rest of his life he continued to mourn her death. Some people he met said it was all he could talk about. For the next few

World War I

Begun on June 28, 1914, the First World War pitted Russia, Britain, Italy and France against Germany, Austria, and what is now Turkey. It was the first "modern" war, with frightening new weapons like machine guns and tanks. Both sides were powerful and well-armed. And neither side was willing to give in. The war dragged on for more than four years; about ten million people died.

When the war started, President Woodrow Wilson was determined to keep the United States out of it. He told people to remain neutral, and he tried to maintain trading and diplomatic relations with both sides. But on May 7, 1915, a German submarine attacked the British ship Lusitania. One hundred and twenty-eight Americans were killed. Then in early 1917, German submarines started sinking all ships bound for Britain, including

American ones. Soon President Wilson, and the United States, had no choice but to join the war. American troops, supplies, and weapons helped turn the tide of the war, and finally, in November 1918, the Germans surrendered and peace was reached.

years, he was sad and unfocused, even though he kept on performing.

Luckily for Harry, Bess was always at his side. She supported Harry through everything. Even when he was perfecting his most dangerous stunts, she never doubted that he would come back to her safe and sound. Sometimes he worried more than she did. Once, right before a bridge jump, he handed a friend a piece of paper that just said “I leave everything to Bess.” He wanted to make sure she would be provided for if something should happen to him.

In April 1917, the United States decided to join the war in Europe. Harry signed up for military service that same month. He was determined to help however he could.

Unfortunately, Harry, now forty-three, was too old to join the army, even though he was in better shape than many younger men. So Harry found other ways to help. Millions of people were willing to pay money to see Harry perform—so why not give some of that money to the war effort?

Harry did shows all across the United States to raise money for American troops. Not only that, he also performed for thousands of soldiers. He did shows for the wounded in army camps. He even taught classes for soldiers before they went off to war, showing them how to escape from German handcuffs and locks. Harry had always guarded his secrets carefully; now he revealed some of them. It was worth it if he could help America win.

"It is not a question of 'will we win' or 'will we lose,'" he wrote. "WE MUST WIN, and that is all there is to it." The Hippodrome benefit alone (where he introduced the Vanishing Elephant) raised nearly ten thousand dollars for families of American soldiers.

All his life Houdini devoted time to what he called "Good Works." These included donating money to hospitals and orphanages, where he also performed for free. Children adored him, and he especially loved doing his show for them.

It always made Harry sad that he and Bess never had

children. It was the one thing missing from their marriage. He was jealous of his brother, Theo, who had sons. But Bess and Harry were happy together anyway. For them, pets became like children. Their dog, Charlie, traveled with them for eight years.

Harry and Bess also had many friends, although he was too busy to have much of a social life. He loved meeting other famous people—especially ones who knew who he was. On one boat trip between Europe and America, he astonished former president Teddy Roosevelt with some of his tricks. For the rest of his life, Harry treasured the photograph he had of the two of them together. There are also photographs of Houdini with Charlie Chaplin and Buster Keaton, two of the greatest comic stars of the silent screen. And Houdini became good friends with Jack London, author of *The Call of the Wild* and *White Fang*. He also met Sir Arthur Conan Doyle, the man who created Sherlock Holmes. But this friendship ended less happily for Harry Houdini.

Chapter 10

So You Want to Be a Detective

Sir Arthur Conan Doyle was an English writer, famous for his bestselling mysteries about the great detective Sherlock Holmes. Holmes was brilliant and observant—he could tell a hundred things about a man just by looking at and listening to him. Sherlock Holmes used logic to solve mysteries, like putting together the pieces of a complicated puzzle. Nobody could fool him. But his creator, Sir Arthur Conan Doyle, was not much like his famous sharp-eyed, suspicious hero.

When Houdini and Conan Doyle met, Sir Arthur had recently become interested in a new movement called "Spiritualism." Spiritualism was very popular after World

War I, in the 1920s. Spiritualists claimed to communicate with ghosts and spirits of the dead. After the war, many people wanted to believe—needed to believe—they could contact their lost loved ones.

At a séance, people calling themselves mediums would gather a group around a table and try to communicate with the dead. Mediums used a lot of mysterious phenomena to show that ghosts were really present … floating objects, strange knocks on the table, instruments that played themselves.

According to Sir Arthur, Spiritualism was "absolutely the most important development in the whole history of the human race." Harry didn't believe a word of it. He knew how talking to the dead worked; it had been a part of his own show when he was very young. But he stopped doing it, because it was wrong to trick people. He was convinced that all these new mediums were fakes, too.

Sir Arthur's belief in Spiritualism appalled Harry. How could such a smart man, with such a respect for logic, be deceived by parlor tricks? The answer is that people believe what they want to believe. Sir Arthur had lost a son in World War I. After a medium delivered a message from his son, Sir Arthur desperately wanted to believe it was true. The Conan Doyles were both so committed to Spiritualism that Lady Conan Doyle started trying to channel spirits herself.

Harry kept quiet about his doubts when he first met Sir Arthur. He wanted to remain friends with the great author. Apart from Spiritualism, the two men really got along very well. Sir Arthur was fascinated by Harry's illusions and skills. Even later in life, after they stopped speaking to each other, Sir Arthur still told people he was sure that Harry had psychic abilities. How else could you explain his escapes? Well, of course, Harry could have explained them, but he wasn't about to reveal his secrets that easily.

The two men first met in 1920, and were close friends for almost two years. But in early 1922, because Harry liked Sir Arthur, he agreed to attend a séance with him. It was a big

Spiritualism

Spiritualism became very popular in the United States in the late 1800s. Two sisters, Margaret and Catherine Fox, claimed that they could hear a ghost in their house. The sisters claimed that they could interpret the ghost's rapping noises that were actually messages from the spirit world. Their sessions with the ghost became performances that people could attend. Soon the girls started touring all across the country, "speaking" with a number of other spirits.

The popularity of the Fox act attracted thousands of people who flocked to what they believed was a new religious movement—Spiritualism. However, Spiritualism suffered a blow in 1888 when Margaret Fox publicly admitted that she and her sister were frauds. They had made the rapping sounds by cracking their toes. She wanted people to know it was all tricks and lies.

But a lot of people refused to believe that Spiritualism was fake. One of these was Sir Arthur Conan Doyle, who insisted that Harry Houdini really had supernatural powers.

mistake.

The Conan Doyles were staying in New Jersey during Sir Arthur's lecture tour of the United States. The Houdinis were visiting for the weekend, and Sir Arthur suggested that they try something called an automatic-writing séance. This meant that Lady Conan Doyle would go into a trance and try to contact the spirits. Then she would write down anything they "told" her. Sir Arthur thought perhaps they would be able to contact Harry's mother.

Harry was nervous about the séance, but he agreed to participate. Perhaps there was some part of him that actually hoped he could communicate with Cecilia. He still missed his mother terribly.

Sir Arthur was thrilled with the results of the séance. His wife filled fifteen pages with messages for Harry, expressing Cecilia's love for him and how much she missed him. Sir Arthur thought Harry had to be as convinced as he was. Surely he couldn't deny this kind of evidence.

Harry didn't want to offend Sir Arthur Conan Doyle. He was polite during the séance and didn't say anything about his suspicions. But afterwards, in his diaries and letters to friends, he openly revealed all his doubts.

For one thing, he said, Lady Conan Doyle had begun the message by drawing a cross at the top of the page. She said this was a typical "sign" showing that the spirit was "good." But Harry did not think his mother, who was Jewish, would ever have drawn a cross. Even more suspicious, the messages were entirely in English—a language Harry's mother had never spoken. Surely if she really wanted to send a message to Harry, she would have written it in German.

Sir Arthur heard about Harry's comments and was outraged. How dare Houdini accuse Sir Arthur's wife of fraud? To be fair, Lady Conan Doyle was probably not trying to trick Houdini. She really might have thought she was receiving messages from Cecilia Weiss. That's how much she believed in Spiritualism and in her own connection to the spirit world.

Harry and Sir Arthur started writing angry letters to each other in April of 1922. The argument quickly moved into the public eye. Newspapers loved the idea of two famous figures quarreling over such a hot issue. They published articles each of them wrote defending his position. On this issue, the two men would always disagree—and it destroyed their friendship.

In the next couple of years, Harry dedicated a great deal of his time to exposing fake mediums and debunking Spiritualists. He even wrote a couple of books about Spiritualism, including *A Magician Among the Spirits*, published in 1924. He challenged anyone to produce some "spirit phenomena" that he could not reproduce using a magician's tricks. If someone did convince him, he offered to pay them $10,000. As in the case of his earlier Handcuff Challenge, he never had to pay up.

He also traveled the country performing an act specially

designed to show everyone how these “mediums” did their tricks. A lot of séances took place in dark rooms, with everyone in a circle holding hands. Harry showed how the medium could use his or her feet and head to create the sounds and effects people heard and saw in the dark. He showed how “psychics” could easily find out information about people to trick them.

Harry sat in on séances all over the USA. He asked the mediums questions that only his mother could answer, saying that if they could really talk to the dead, they would surely be able to get the answer from her. Sometimes he even disguised himself, since a lot of mediums refused to perform a séance with Houdini in the room.

It is possible that Harry really wanted to find a true medium. He would have given anything to be able to speak to his mother just once more. If he had found anyone who convinced him, he said he was willing to admit it. But Harry thought it was terrible to make people, who were often heartbroken and vulnerable, pay for lies and deception. Exposing these frauds was another way Harry felt he was helping people.

Chapter 11

So You Want to Be Remembered Forever

A lot of people think that Harry died during one of his difficult escapes. In fact, there is a movie about his life (mostly fictional), made in 1953, called *Houdini*, in which he drowns during one of his daredevil stunts. His escapes certainly were dangerous and could have caused his death. But that's not what happened.

On the morning of October 22, 1926, Harry was at McGill University in Montreal, Canada. A few days earlier, he had fractured his ankle during an escape. Houdini was limping, tired, and under stress because Bess was suffering from food poisoning. But no matter how bad he felt, nothing would stop him from performing.

Harry was relaxing in his dressing room, having his portrait drawn, when a student from the university knocked and came in. He started asking Harry questions about himself—about his life and beliefs, and, of course, his tricks. Harry was friendly, even though he was tired.

At one point, the student said, "Is it true, Mr. Houdini, that you are so strong, a man could hit you in the stomach, and it wouldn't hurt you?"

Harry was very strong. But more importantly, he knew what to do with his muscles so that he wouldn't get hurt when somebody hit him. It took a moment of preparation and tightening his stomach. So when the student asked if he could try hitting him, Harry said sure. Unfortunately, Harry wasn't really paying attention. Before he had a chance to prepare himself, the visitor started punching him really hard in the stomach.

"Hey, stop that!" the other people in the room gasped. "Are you insane?"

Harry raised his hand, and the student stopped. "That will do," said Harry weakly.

Harry was in a lot of pain. What he didn't know was that the man had accidentally ruptured Harry's appendix. Harry was in serious danger. But he still refused to cancel his shows. He was Harry Houdini. He wasn't going to let a little stomach pain keep him down.

Harry performed his last show in Detroit on the night of October 24, and then collapsed. Bess insisted on taking him to the hospital, and on October 25 the doctors removed his appendix. Sadly, it was too late for Harry. He had developed a very bad infection from the injury. Harry fought to stay alive for several more days. Finally, he told his brother, Theo, "I'm tired of fighting ... I can't fight any more." Those were his last words.

Harry died on Halloween—October 31, 1926. He was fifty-two years old. After a huge funeral attended by thousands of people, Harry was buried next to his mother in Machpelah

Cemetery, in the New York City borough of Queens.

For years Bess tried to contact Harry's ghost. He had promised her that if it was at all possible to come back and talk to the living, he would find a way to contact her. He even told her a secret message that would let her know it was him for real. But the message never came.

Bess lived for many more years, but she never forgot Harry, and she spent the rest of her life keeping his memory alive.

So what was the magic of Harry Houdini really all about? How did he do his amazing tricks? Well, we do know about some of them. "Metamorphosis" and the "Milk Can Escape" were mostly mechanical—half the trick was in the apparatus he used. Even so, it would be hard (and very dangerous) to duplicate Harry's act. He really could have had a fatal accident doing most of his escapes. But it didn't matter to him. He loved performing, and he loved being famous. He also loved being the only person in the world who could do these tricks.

Harry was born in a time of new discoveries and inventions. He loved the modern world, and his life showed that love—whether it was airplanes, movies, or the triumph of science over Spiritualism. If he lived today, he would probably have been the first performer to have his own website, and he would be trying to figure out ways to escape from a space shuttle.

As a young boy, Harry was one of the millions of people who came to America hoping to make their dreams come true. He spent his life following his dream and put all his energy into everything he did. He showed that anyone can do anything through hard work and believing in himself.

There is a lot of mystery about Harry Houdini even today. People wonder—was there a big secret to his magic that nobody ever knew? Harry liked to make people think so. And some of his tricks are almost impossible to explain. But as Bess always said: it was never really about the tricks. Harry's magic was all in the man, Harry Houdini himself.

Timeline of Houdini's Life

1874 — Harry (Ehrich Weiss) is born, March 24, in Budapest, Hungary.

1878 — Harry and his family move to America.

1886 — Harry runs away from home.

1887 — Harry moves to New York City with his father.

1890 — Harry reads *The Memoirs of Robert-Houdin* and is inspired to become a magician.

1892 — Harry's father, Rabbi Mayer Samuel Weiss, dies on October 5.

1893 — Harry and his brother Theo perform at the World's Fair in Chicago.

1894 — Harry meets and marries Beatrice (Bess) Raymond.

1899 — Harry is discovered by Martin Beck and starts performing in vaudeville houses.

1900 — Harry and Bess sail to England for European tour.

1902 — Harry is challenged by William Hodgson in England.

1905 — Harry and Bess return to America.

1908 — Harry's milk can trick premieres.

1910 — Harry becomes the first person to fly an airplane in Australia.

1913 — Harry's mother, Cecilia Weiss, dies on July 17.

1918 — Harry performs the Vanishing Elephant trick in New York City.

1919 — Harry's first movie, *The Master Mystery*, opens.

1922 — Harry attends the séance that ends his friendship with Sir Arthur Conan Doyle.

1924 — Harry's book *A Magician Among the Spirits* is published.

1926 — Harry dies on October 31.

Timeline of the World

1874	First exhibit of Impressionist paintings is held in Paris.
1879	Albert Einstein is born.
1886	The Statue of Liberty is dedicated.
1887	Sir Arthur Conan Doyle publishes the first Sherlock Holmes story.
1891	Basketball is invented in Massachusetts.
1892	Ellis Island opens in New York harbor.
1893	New Zealand becomes the first country in the world that allows women to vote.
1894	Rudyard Kipling publishes *The Jungle Book.*
1899	The Brooklyn Children's Museum opens as the world's first children's museum.
1900	Dr. Sigmund Freud publishes *The Interpretation of Dreams.*
1902	First *Tyrannosaurus rex* fossil is discovered.
	Beatrix Potter publishes the first Peter Rabbit story.
1904	The New York City subway opens.
1908	Henry Ford develops the first Model T automobile and sells it for $850.
1910	Boy Scouts of America is incorporated.
1913	First crossword puzzle appears in NY *World* newspaper.
1922	Lincoln Memorial is dedicated.
	King Tutankhamen's tomb is discovered.
1923	Rin-Tin-Tin becomes the first dog movie star.
1926	Annie Oakley dies.